PROTECTING CHILDREN AND YOUNG PEOPLE

Child Maltreatment and High Risk Families

Protecting Children and Young People series

Sharon Vincent, *Learning from Child Deaths and Serious Abuse in Scotland* (2010)

Anne Stafford, Sharon Vincent and Nigel Parton (eds) *Child Protection Reform across the United Kingdom* (2010)

Kate Alexander and Anne Stafford, *Children and Organised Sport* (2011)

Sharon Vincent, *Preventing Child Deaths: Learning from Review* (2013)

Caroline Bradbury-Jones, *Children as Co-researchers: The Need for Protection* (2014)

Sharon Vincent (ed.), *Early Intervention: Supporting and Strengthening Families* (2015)

See www.dunedinacademicpress.co.uk for details of all our publications

Editorial Advisory Board

Professor Marian Brandon, The School of Social Work and Psychology, University of East Anglia

Dr Anne Lazenbatt, School of Sociology, Social Policy and Social Work, Queen's University Belfast

Professor Tarja Pösö, School of Social Sciences and Humanities, University of Tampere

Professor Wendy Rose, Faculty of Health and Social Care, The Open University

Professor Trevor Spratt, Director of the Children's Research Centre, Trinity College Dublin

PROTECTING CHILDREN AND YOUNG PEOPLE
SERIES EDITORS
JOHN DEVANEY
School of Sociology, Social Policy and Social Work, Queen's
University Belfast
and JULIE TAYLOR
University of Edinburgh, Child Protection Research Centre
and SHARON VINCENT
Centre for Health and Social Care Improvement, University of
Wolverhampton

Child Maltreatment and High Risk Families

Julie Taylor
NSPCC Chair in Child Protection,
University of Edinburgh

Anne Lazenbatt
NSPCC Reader in Childhood Studies,
Queen's University of Belfast

EDINBURGH ◆ LONDON

Published by Dunedin Academic Press Ltd

Head Office: Hudson House, 8 Albany Street, Edinburgh EH1 3QB
London Office: 352 Cromwell Tower, Barbican, London EC2Y 8NB

ISBNs
978–1–78046–031–4 (Paperback)
978–1–78046–519–7 (eBook)
978–1–78046–524–1 (Kindle)

ISSN: 1756–0691

British Library Cataloguing in Publication data
A catalogue record for this book is available at the British Library

Typeset by Makar Publishing Production
Printed in Great Britain by CPI Antony Rowe

CONTENTS

ACKNOWLEDGEMENTS

This book started life as a scoping report for the physical abuse in high risk families theme at the NSPCC in 2010. Particular thanks are due to Di Jerwood (National Society for the Prevention of Cruelty to Children – NSPCC) and Anna Anderson (University of Edinburgh).

LIST OF ABBREVIATIONS

AAP	American Academy of Pediatrics
ACMD	Advisory Council on the Misuse of Drugs
ASFA	Adoption and Safe Families Act 1997
CBT	Cognitive behavioural therapy
CPR	Child-protection register
CPS	Crown Prosecution Service
EBD	Eco-bio-developmental
FAS	Foetal Alcohol Syndrome
FGC	Female genital cutting
FGM	Female genital mutilation
FII	Fabricated and Induced Illness
HPA	Hypothalamic–pituitary–adrenal axis
MRI	Magnetic resonance imaging
NAHI	Non-accidental head injury
NFP	Nurse-Family Partnership
NSPCC	National Society for the Prevention of Cruelty to Children
PCIT	Parent-Child Interaction Therapy
PET	Positron emission tomography
PTSD	Post-Traumatic Stress Disorder
RCT	Randomised Controlled Trial
SBS	Shaken Baby Syndrome
SCR	Serious Case Review
SEEK	Safe Environment for Every Kid

INTRODUCTION

Today child maltreatment is seen as a major and complex public health and social welfare problem, caused by a range of factors that involve the individual, the family and the community. Child abuse or neglect and general trauma, including the witnessing of domestic violence, are alarmingly common, and pose major threats and risks to child health and well-being (Scannapieco and Connell-Carrick, 2005). Such behaviour can alter normal child development and, without intervention, can have lifelong consequences (Flaherty *et al.*, 2008) including death. Child abuse includes any type of maltreatment or harm inflicted on children and young people through interactions with adults (or older adolescents). These include, in decreasing level of frequency: neglect; physical abuse and non-accidental injury; emotional, psychological abuse or bullying; and sexual abuse (Radford *et al.*, 2011). However, to define child abuse operationally is a complex task, as it involves an interpretation of what acts or behaviours towards a child are inappropriate and an estimation of the amount of harm suffered by a child. There are specific criminal laws which provide a clear benchmark of what is inappropriate behaviour, such as the rape of a child. But in other instances the civil law focuses on whether the child has suffered harm as a consequence of parental behaviour (or inaction in the case of neglect), and whether the harm is significant or not, such as when concerns exist about parental substance misuse or domestic violence. Clearly, it is always difficult to estimate the incidence and prevalence of a phenomenon such as child abuse. This is partly due to the difficulty in defining 'child abuse', but it is also related to the hidden nature of abuse and the varied forms in which it can present. Our understanding of the nature of child abuse comes from a range of sources, including statistics gathered by professionals in the course of their work, personal accounts provided by survivors of abuse and neglect, and research studies.

We know that sustained maltreatment can have major, long-term effects on all aspects of children's health, as well as on their growth, intellectual development and mental well-being; moreover, it can impair their functioning as adults (Kendall-Tackett, 2002). Indeed, evidence tells us that all forms of child maltreatment should be considered important risks to overall health and a sizeable impact on the major contributors to the global burden of disease (Norman *et al.*, 2012). Nevertheless, the public and many professionals remain unaware of these long-term health and mental health effects on infants and children (Gilbert *et al.*, 2009). There has perhaps been some complacency in the professional and public eye over the last few years surrounding the topic of child abuse. Firstly, for most people it seems inconceivable that something we have known about for so long is still happening on such an unimaginable scale. That children should still be burnt and beaten, neglected or sexually abused on a daily basis does not seem congruent with modern society (Bonomi *et al.*, 2008a; 2008b). Children may be at risk of experiencing harm from a range of people: for example, parents; siblings; extended family members; family friends; peers; adults in positions of trust; and strangers. Contrary to some media representations, children are at most risk from those who are known to them, rather than strangers. Whatever the relationship, there is a very small group of individuals who pose a significant risk to any child with whom they may have contact. Since this is the case, recent improvements in the criminal justice-led arrangements for monitoring and managing adults who pose a risk to children are essential in complementing the child-protection system. Secondly, we know that almost all child abuse occurs within families who are known to have one or more risk factors present, and that most child maltreatment occurs within a context of 'high risk families'. This context of 'high risk' is usually the accumulation of various risk factors, rather than the presence of any single one that affects outcomes. It is probably best understood by analysing the complex interactions between the numbers of risk factors that interconnect at different levels in an individual's life.

We now know that child abuse is far more common than suggested by official statistics of children assessed by child-protection services. Every year around one in ten children (about one million children in the UK) are maltreated, but official statistics indicate that less than one-tenth of this burden is investigated and substantiated. A UK population-based survey showed that 7% of individuals aged 18–33 years had been subject to serious physical abuse at the hands of a parent or carer (Brooker *et al.*, 2001). Physical abuse is a particularly significant problem in babies under the age of one year, since very young babies have the highest risk of suffering damage or death as a result of such abuse (Lazenbatt *et al.*, 2012). The most comprehensive figures on the prevalence of child abuse in the UK were collected by the National Society for the Prevention of Cruelty to Children (NSPCC) in their 2009 study of child maltreatment (Radford *et al.*, 2011). This study was undertaken with a random probability sample of parents, young people and young adults from across the UK, and the participants were interviewed about their experiences of child abuse and neglect. The sample consisted of: 2,160 parents or guardians of children aged less than eleven years; 2,275 young people aged 11–17 years with additional information from their parents or guardians; and 1,761 young adults aged 18–24 years. One in four of the young adults in this study reported having experienced severe maltreatment in childhood. (This was defined as severe physical and emotional abuse by any adult, severe neglect by parents or guardians and/or contact sexual abuse by any adult or peer.) Over the past six years in the UK there has been a substantial increase in the numbers of children assessed by professionals as being at risk of experiencing harm through abuse and neglect. Based on the evidence from prevalence research (Radford *et al.*, 2011), this is more likely to reflect an increased awareness and identification of children at risk of experiencing harm rather than a rise in the numbers suffering abuse and neglect.

Although child maltreatment can occur in any family, it is most often concentrated in families vulnerable to a combination of more complex risk factors. Many of these risk factors for abuse are multiple and interact to produce an even greater risk to families. We know that child maltreatment can take many forms, and this book is designed to explore in more detail some of the effects for children within 'high risk' families where parents are living with combinations of domestic abuse, drug and alcohol misuse and mental illness. The consequences for children are that they may be:

- witnessing violence or becoming part of a violent activity;
- experiencing the physical effects of violence such as fractures, non-accidental head injury, abusive head trauma, physical punishment;
- neglected;
- suffering female genital mutilation;
- involved in fabricated and induced illness;
- involved in revenge killing; or
- suffering from the major effects of the accompanying psychological and emotional abuse.

These risks factors can significantly affect infant and child health and the long-term emotional development and well-being of children. Indeed, over time such childhood adversities may manifest themselves in the experience of homelessness, unemployment, imprisonment, drug and alcohol addiction, physical and mental-health problems and even early death. Understanding why this is so involves an examination of the effects of early stress on human physiology (Glaser, 2007). Evidence shows that 'the cumulative exposure of these risks on the developing brain is an activated stress response' (Anda and Brown, 2010) that links these various forms of maltreatment and adverse health consequences, which then trigger a stress or anxiety response. This response can influence the nervous and immune systems causing alteration of the function of the hypothalamic–pituitary–adrenal (HPA) axis (Widom and Maxfield, 2001; Glaser, 2002; Neigh *et al.*, 2009). Indeed these cumulative risks may impact on the developing child to cause: '… lasting alterations in stress responsive neurobiological systems, and these lasting effects on the developing brain would be expected to affect numerous human functions into adulthood, including emotional regulation, somatic signal processing, substance abuse, sexuality, memory arousal, and aggression'. Early exposure to stress and trauma causes physical effects on an infant's neurodevelopment, which may lead to changes in their long-term response to stress and vulnerability or later mental-health disorders (De Bellis and Thomas, 2003; De Bellis, 2005; Glaser, 2007; Cicchetti, 2014).

This book also aims: to increase our understanding of how we identify these risks to children and families before it is too late; to assess the impacts of these risks on children and families; to high-light the learning we have gained from evidence-based practice and research; and to view the current landscape of service delivery in rela-tion to child abuse within 'high risk families'. There are overwhelming moral, ethical, economic and ecological reasons why this topic should be of paramount concern. The scale of the problem alone suggests that families living in high risk situations that lead to child maltreat-ment are displaying significant issues within all four countries of the UK.[1] The costs, both direct [e.g. medical care] and indirect [e.g. crimi-nal justice] of addressing these consequences are enormous (Browne *et al.*, 2007). In Europe only the UK has attempted to calculate the total economic burden of maltreatment. In 1996 this was estimated at £735 million (National Commission of Inquiry into the Prevention of Child Abuse, 1996). More recent work is likely to demonstrate even more significant costs.

There are also significant costs to children's lives. Children are still dying from abuse in spite of the best efforts of those working within the child protection system. Child deaths as a result of abuse and neglect remain a serious problem across nations (UNICEF, 2003). While the deaths of children through illness and accidents have been closely monitored, those resulting from maltreatment are more difficult to ascertain because the perpetrators, usually parents and carers, are less likely to be forthcoming about the circumstances due to the inevitable legal consequences and public outcry (Pritchard and Sharples, 2008; Pritchard and Williams, 2010). It is estimated that approximately 3,500 children under the age of fifteen die annually in industrialised nations as a result of abuse. The United Nations esti-mate that every week two children die from abuse and neglect in the UK and Germany, three in France, four in Japan, and twenty-seven in the United States. The risk of death by maltreatment is approximately three times greater for the under-ones than for those aged 1 to 4, who in turn face double the risk of those aged 5 to 14 (UNICEF, 2003).

Even in the womb, children require parents who will provide for their physical, social and emotional needs, through the expression of love, a sense of security and the provision of care (Barker *et al.* 2002). Children, especially when they are younger, depend on par-ents and family to provide the stability and security required to form meaningful attachments and to grow and develop in ways which are positive. However, we also know that not all parents provide this sense of stability and safety, either because they are unable or unwilling to do so. There is a fine judgement to be achieved in ensuring that a child's right to be kept safe is balanced with the right of parents to bring up their child without undue interference by the state. However, infants and children are likely to be most at risk of significant abuse when there is a cumulative interaction of a number of the following risk factors within the family (Vincent, 2010; Vincent and Petch, 2010):

- presence of a violent man in the household;
- parental conflict and/or domestic violence and abuse;
- parental/carer mental ill health;
- parental/carer substance misuse;
- parental/carer learning disability;
- associated poverty/financial problems;
- poverty and financial difficulties;
- housing difficulties or frequent house moves;
- criminal convictions;
- young parents;
- social isolation/poor support networks;
- parental/carer experience of abuse and/or care in childhood;
- long-term involvement with agencies; or
- withdrawal from contact with the outside world.

The following children might be more likely to die or experience serious abuse (Devaney *et al.*, 2011):

- very young children;
- only or youngest child in family;
- children who have previously experienced neglect, physical or emotional abuse;
- children with special needs;
- hard-to-help teenagers

We also know that child maltreatment is one of the most serious events undermining healthy psychological development, and no other social risk factor has a stronger association with developmental psychopathology (Brooker *et al.*, 2001; Perry, 2001). Importantly, the use of a developmental psychopathology perspective has provided evidence to increase our understanding of the causes and consequences of child maltreatment (Cicchetti and Toth, 2005; Cicchetti *et al.,* 2006). The introduction of treatments along the child's developmental trajectory has highlighted the processes that result in resilient functioning in some maltreated children despite their having experienced adversity (Cicchetti and Manley, 1990; Cicchetti, 2013). The negative sequelae in others have been documented across a range of domains including cognition, language, learning, socio-emotional development, and mental and physical health (Cicchetti and Manley, 1990). There is a sizeable literature documenting a relationship between all types of child maltreatment and a variety of negative health and mental-health consequences, including biological, psychological, and social deficits (for reviews, see Crittenden, 1998; Kendall-Tackett, 2001; 2003). However, the process by which maltreatment leads to negative health outcomes, including the causal role of maltreatment, is not fully understood. This is primarily because of the lack of well-developed theory and methodologically rigorous studies examining factors related to child maltreatment. Many studies have employed cross-sectional designs in comparing the health of individuals who report child maltreatment with those who do not (Felitti *et al.,* 1998). However, more longitudinal studies are needed to better examine the processes by which maltreatment leads to negative outcomes. Aside from the serious physical and health consequences of child maltreatment, several emotional and behavioural consequences for children have been noted in the literature (Cicchetti, 2014). These consequences vary according to differences in the severity, duration, and frequency of maltreatment, as well as differences in the child [e.g., temperament, coping skills, developmental stage] and the child's environment [e.g., family income, social support, neighbourhood characteristics] (Hecht and Hansen, 2001). Obviously, however, sustained maltreatment can have major long-term effects on all aspects of children's health and well-being.

Dealing with high risk families is an overwhelming task and as such it can be difficult to know where to start. As yet, there are no well-developed explanatory models for child abuse, nor do we know enough about gender interaction and genetic and environmental influences. It is usually the accumulation of risk rather than the presence of any single risk factor that affects outcomes (Devaney *et al.*, in press). Certainly the 'toxic trio' of domestic abuse, substance misuse and parental mental ill health provide a milieu of most risk, but we do not know enough about the relative weightings of each and within this there is a need to separate alcohol and substance dependencies (Anda and Brown 2010). Beginning to identify risk factors, though, is not the same as being able to predict which families may harm their children. Recently, ecological models such as those of Bronfenbrenner (Bronfenbrenner, 1979) have been accepted as useful in examining risk factors for child maltreatment, by conceptualising maltreatment as having interacting and multiple determinants that can occur in the individual, in the family, and in the community and culture. Therefore children living in poverty and deprivation continue to be at a higher risk of a wide range of adverse experiences and unfavourable outcomes, including maltreatment and most notably physical abuse and neglect by parents. The main influence of poverty on parenting appears to be the stress it causes, which in turn disrupts parenting practices. The quality of the neighbourhood is also crucial as are the risks from limited income and poor parental education although their importance varies with the type of maltreatment (Sidebotham and Golding, 2001; May-Chahal *et al.*, 2004; Sidebotham and Fleming, 2007). Strong evidence suggests a clear pathway by which parental drug and alcohol problems can cause child maltreatment in individual families but evidence for a causal link within populations is less certain. However, substance misuse is undoubtedly a common factor in incidents involving both spouse and child maltreatment (Scottish Government, 2013).

Numerous studies have demonstrated the negative effects that child maltreatment can have throughout the lifetime and that these effects have the potential to affect both parenting behaviours and the parenting environment. However, inter-generational transmission of abuse is not inevitable and the majority of physically abused individuals are not violent towards their own children (Rutter, 2006; Murray and Zautra, 2012; Ungar, 2013). Further, a deficit model focusing only on risk and harm is not useful. Finding known and new ways to foster resilience and bolster protective factors is crucial. A public health approach directly addresses the call to move away from traditional responses that aim to prevent recurrence of maltreatment to preventing it happening at all, while simultaneously acknowledging the importance of a full spectrum of action that might require a differential response.

This book will also illustrate how overall there is a striking lack of empirically and theoretically sound evaluation of interventions within the field of child maltreatment. A broad range of programmes for prevention of child maltreatment exist, however, the effectiveness of most of these programmes is unknown (MacMillan *et al.*, 2009). Although this provides promise in a number of interventions, it is not always possible to draw inferences specifically. While our knowledge about the kinds of harm done to children has expanded there are still many gaps in our understanding of why they are harmed, which circumstances are mostly likely to give rise to harming, what can be done to prevent it and what will most help in recovery in the longer term. A number of rigorous systematic reviews have shed light on what might be effective interventions for child abuse (Montgomery *et al.*, 2009; Norman *et al.*, 2012), although we probably know more about the limitations of our knowledge. Designing and evaluating interventions within a public health framework (Hardiker *et al.*, 1991; Butchart *et al.*, 2006) that prevent child maltreatment is essential. In this way a clear and operational definition of child maltreatment as a 'problem' can be developed; an identification of the risk and protective factors and any causal links can be ascertained; measures of intervention effectiveness can be employed to include a process evaluation and measures of short-term outcomes; and finally the implementation of an intervention with ongoing evaluation and monitoring to provide evidence of effectiveness and sustainability in the longer term. MacMillan and colleagues (MacMillan *et al.*, 2008) suggest that too often, interventions are implemented before undergoing adequate evaluation and the term 'promising' is sometimes misinterpreted as sufficient evidence for widespread dissemination. However one systematic review (Norman *et al.*, 2012) suggests a causal relationship between non-sexual child maltreatment and a range of mental disorders, drug, use, suicide attempts, sexually transmitted infections and risky sexual behaviour. This awareness of the long-term and lasting effects of child abuse makes the identification of those at risk and the development of sound evaluation frameworks for interventions that are effective for children all the more important.

Over recent years there has been an upsurge in research that has increased our knowledge and understanding of how pregnancy and the first postnatal year can lay significant foundations for positive child development. Child abuse and maltreatment can have an impact early in an infant's life, even as early as pregnancy and the postpartum period and can affect infants' physical and emotional health, their learning and their capacity to form positive relationships throughout their lives (Lazenbatt, 2010). Infants are an especially vulnerable group to maltreatment because they are almost completely dependent on others for their physical, emotional and cognitive development and, ultimately, their survival. This new knowledge has created a consensus of opinion about the need to develop early interventions to help young children get the best start in life. Around 198,000 babies under one year of age in the UK are living within a 'high risk' family and have parents who are affected by domestic violence, substance misuse or mental-health problems (Manning *et al.*, 2009). An analysis of Serious Case Reviews (SCRs) in England shows that at least one of these three issues is present in many cases, and there is often a high degree of overlap of these factors in cases of child death and serious injury (Ofsted, 2011a). There is as yet no definitive explanation for this high incidence, though frailty and total dependence are important features. However, the very real demands and stresses placed on a family by a newborn baby are almost certainly a factor.

Detrimental early experiences and subsequent neuro-developmental damage, can cause an infant to develop a range of problems, such as language delay, lack of empathy, hyperactivity associated with disruptive behaviour and distractibility or hyper-vigilance (Angst *et al.*, 2011; Norman *et al.*, 2012), as well as emotional difficulties stemming from poor impulse control and a lack of compassion (Schore, 2001). Infants and toddlers are at greatest risk of serious injury and are often the most difficult cases to recognise because of absence of available history from the victim (Woodman *et al.*, 2011). Physical abuse is associated with various types of injuries and lack of secure parental attachments, particularly when exposure to such abuse occurs in the first three or four years of life (Vinchon *et al.*, 2005). It is estimated that 10% of admissions to paediatric burns and plastic surgery units are related to child maltreatment (Chester *et al.*, 2006).

Adolescence is also a particular and very important stage of human development, generally occurring between puberty and legal adulthood (typically between the ages of 11 years and 18 years). During adolescence young people undergo significant physiological, psychological and social change: negotiating puberty; completing growth; assuming a sexually dimorphic body shape; developing new cognitive skills; developing and maintaining intimate relationships outside the family; learning to manage a range of complex emotions; thinking independently; and problem solving. Maltreatment for adolescents is particularly related to a variety of serious consequences, including substance use, violence, health-risking sex behaviours, depression, obesity and eating disorders, internalising problems, and school disengagement (Gilbert *et al.*, 2009). Most importantly previous research has demonstrated that a connection between childhood abuse and suicide exists (Glowinski *et al.*, 2001). In a large and representative research study (Bruffaerts *et al.*, 2010) it was revealed that both physical and sexual abuse were strongly related with suicidal risk behaviour. Another study found that a history of childhood maltreatment is likely to play a key role in the onset and recurrence of suicide attempts (Perroud *et al.*, 2007). Research suggests that abuse and neglect doubles the risk of attempted suicide for adolescents (Evans *et al.*, 2005; Brodsky and Stanley, 2008). The systematic review by Evans *et al.* (2005) found a strong link between physical/sexual abuse and attempted suicide/suicidal thoughts occurring during adolescence. The authors suggested that sexual abuse could be specifically related to suicidal behaviour because it is closely associated with feelings of shame and internal attributions of blame (Brodsky and Stanley, 2008).

There is also some evidence to suggest that witnessing violence in the home or elsewhere also contributes to an increased risk for suicidal behaviour (Dube *et al.*, 2001). An adolescent witnessing domestic violence may have an increased risk of suicidal behaviour, and are more likely to self-harm (Anda and Brown, 2010). Suicide is usually preceded by antisocial behaviour, such as inappropriate use of alcohol or engaging in high risk behaviours such as staying away from home or coming into conflict with the law. Older children who witness violence between their parents are at a greater risk for developing antisocial behaviours (Fergusson and Horwood, 1998), which in turn can lead to suicide or suicide attempts in adolescence. The immediacy of the stress and pain of witnessing domestic violence are experiences not easily escaped by adolescents, and this makes suicide appear to be the only solution to a problem that they cannot control (Anda and Brown, 2010). The relationship between domestic violence and suicide attempts among adults demonstrates how these childhood exposures have a long-term impact on the risk of suicide attempts.

Some key features of effective interventions can be extrapolated however, with the most promising evidence coming from parenting interventions such as Webster-Stratton's Incredible Years, Parent-Child Interaction Therapy, abusive head trauma programmes and a number of others. It is not always possible to draw inferences, as these home-visiting programmes are not uniformly effective and more rigorous evaluation programmes and replication are required. The Nurse-Family Partnership developed by David Olds provides intensive visitation by nurses during a woman's pregnancy and the first two years after birth appears to have the best evidence (Krugman *et al.*, 2007). The Family Nurse Partnership (FNP as it is known in the UK) is being tested currently in UK settings cross the four nations through a number of randomised controlled trials (Allen, 2011a,b), and Nottingham City's Early Intervention Model is now commonly cited as a model of best practice (Allen, 2011b). Although area based interventions or group-based interventions such as FNP, which targets single mothers, have been shown to be effective, Lea's (2011) review of interventions with families with complex needs suggests that the most effective interventions for addressing multiple needs tend to be those that are targeted at specific populations; and usually work with both parents and children, building resilience and ensuring positive change for the future. Lea (2011) also stresses the importance of whole family approaches with public health components integrated and coordinated practice approaches to meeting the needs of families with complex needs such as domestic abuse, drug misuse and parental mental-health problems.

While our knowledge about the kinds of harm done to children has expanded, this book illustrates that there are still many gaps in our understanding of why they are harmed, which circumstances are mostly likely to give rise to these, what can be done to prevent harm (upstream) and what will most help in recovery downstream. Identifying those gaps provides the platform on which research, practice and policy can build. The book chapters expand on the knowledge we already know and illustrate the effects of maltreatment in high risk families through a child's developmental stages. Finally and most importantly, evidence shows us that it is possible to prevent abuse and neglect and that infancy and the early years of a child's life are a window of opportunity for preventative interventions, for developing stronger infant-parent relationships and a crucial time to reduce later emotional, psychological and developmental difficulties. The health risks of abuse and the burden placed on health systems and society illustrates the need to stop abuse before it starts through primary prevention efforts. The book finished by stressing that the availability of appropriate treatments to meet the needs of these infants still remains a challenge (Brandon and Thoburn, 2008) and that enhancing the prospects for the development of health and well-being in the lives of maltreated infants requires attention to enhancing opportunities for positive, non-violent family and peer interactions. Developing effective non-stigmatising primary interventions and services is vital in order to promote stronger infant-parent relationships and support parents in meeting their children's health and well-being needs (Barlow *et al.,* 2006).

An explanatory note about the scope of this book is needed as child maltreatment in 'high risk families' is an extremely broad area. It is sometimes difficult to separate the issue of high risk families from that of the maltreatment itself. Many of the interventions for high risk families are equally relevant to other forms of abuse and neglect. There are particular issues of abuse such as trafficking and exploitation, 'honour' killings etc. that have been omitted as these are specifically covered by others in greater detail than could be covered here. However their relevance is acknowledged. Moreover the primary emphasis of the book is on physical abuse, but neglect is a particular feature of high risk families as well, and indeed is the most common form of maltreatment in both the UK and USA. Sexual abuse as well does not sit completely outside high risk families and while there are some unique demarcations from other forms of abuse, it is acknowledged that there is much overlap. Moreover multiple forms of abuse and trauma are common. While children are more likely to die from physical abuse than from either neglect or sexual abuse, many of those children will have been subject to sustained maltreatment, very often neglect, for long periods before the fatal event. Our intention is to focus attention here on high risk families and violence and refer readers to other authoritative books for more detail on other forms of harm.

This introductory chapter has set the scene for the content and scope of the book. Child maltreatment is common, and poses risks to the long-term health and development of children and young people, risks of which the public are often unaware and that professionals can minimise. Although a small number of people pose risks to children, almost all maltreatment occurs in families where one or more risk factors is present. This 'high risk' context is generally cumulative and multi-layered, with a complex interplay between multiple risk factors that interconnect. In particular, combinations of domestic abuse, parental mental ill health and substance misuse make children and young people most vulnerable, but there are many other risk factors that may be present within the family as well. The early years and adolescence are particularly critical times for children and young people. Dealing with high risk families can be an overwhelming task, fraught with gaps in the evidence and a lack of clear explanatory models. But the long-term consequences of abuse exact an enormous toll on individuals and on society and we need to find more effective ways to support parents in meetings children's needs.

CHAPTER 1

The case for focusing on high risk families

Introduction

In this chapter we set out the case for concentrating on high risk families. We particularly focus on domestic abuse and the impact this has on children and young people. We then turn to parental mental-health challenges and the effects this can sometimes have on children. Parental substance misuse is then examined in some detail. Finally, we turn to other risk factors that are thought to impact on adequate parenting.

> Children living in families with multiple risks are more likely to have long-term disadvantageous cognitive, behavioural and mental-health consequences (Sabates and Dex, 2012).

We know that child abuse or neglect and general trauma, including witnessing domestic violence, are major threats to child health and well-being, altering normal child development and, without intervention, causing lifelong consequences (Anda *et al.*, 2006; Flaherty *et al.*, 2009). These early adversities also make adults more vulnerable to stress and stress-related conditions such as alcohol and substance misuse (Felitti, 2002; Leeb *et al.*, 2011), and can increase the incidence of parental mental-health conditions and the severity of post-traumatic stress disorder (PTSD) and other anxiety disorders (Neigh *et al.*, 2009). Child maltreatment is a major and complex public health and social welfare problem, caused by a myriad of factors that involve the individual, the family and the community. The idea that multiple stressors combine and accumulate in various ways that lead to more deleterious and less reversible outcomes is a common one in the developmental literature (Felitti *et al.*, 1998; Turner *et al.*, 2010). Serious Case Reviews undertaken in the UK in various guises when a child dies from maltreatment also highlight that no single factor causes children to be maltreated, rather a 'toxic trio' of risk factors such as parental mental illness, domestic abuse and drug and alcohol misuse, can increase the risk of neglect or abuse (Brandon *et al.*, 2009). Around 198,000 babies under one in the UK are living in vulnerable and complex family situations with parents who are affected by domestic abuse, substance misuse or mental-health problems (Manning *et al.*, 2009). Also an analysis of SCRs shows that at least one of these three issues is present in many cases, and there is often a high degree of overlap of these 'high risk' factors in cases of child death and serious injury (Ofsted, 2011b). Note though that SCRs represent a minority of cases, most of which may be atypical. There is as yet no definitive explanation for this high incidence, though frailty and total dependence are important. Also the very real demands and stresses placed on a family by a newborn baby are almost certainly a factor. Persistent infant crying can also present a major challenge for many parents and is recognised as a primary trigger for the physical abuse of young children (Barr *et al.*, 2009).

The following sections will concentrate particularly on this 'toxic trio' of domestic abuse, parental mental ill health and substance misuse. However we note that while these are areas that (especially in combination) are hugely dangerous for children, there are other risk factors that may be equally noxious, but we do not yet know enough about them (Jütte *et al.*, 2013).

DOMESTIC ABUSE

Domestic abuse (also referred to as domestic violence or intimate partner violence in the literature) is a major public and social problem, the prevalence and universality of which is well documented (Krug *et al.*, 2002; World Health Organization/London School of Hygiene and Tropical Medicine, 2010). It is a serious infringement of victims' human rights with a range of often serious health implications for women and their children (Feder *et al.*, 2009). Domestic abuse can be physically, emotionally, psychologically and socially devastating to women and can have similarly devastating effects on their infants and children (McGee, 2000; Coker *et al.*, 2002; Osofsky, 2003; Osofsky *et al.*, 2004; Devaney, 2009; Cleaver *et al.*, 2011; Lazenbatt, 2012). Its prevalence in society is shocking and unacceptable, with on average throughout the world one in four of women experiencing domestic abuse at some point in their lives (Ellsberg *et al.*, 2008). The term 'domestic abuse' is used to describe violence perpetrated by an adult against another with whom they have or have had a sexual relationship. This abuse can take many forms including the physical (hitting, kicking, restraining), the sexual (including assault, coercion, female genital mutilation), the psychological (verbal bullying, undermining, social isolation) and the financial (withholding money, or demanding unrealistic expectations with the household budget). The Home Office (Home Office, 2010) definition is: 'Any incident of threatening behaviour, violence or abuse (psychological, physical, sexual, financial or emotional) between adults who are or have been intimate partners or family members, regardless of gender or sexuality.' This includes issues of particular concern to black and minority ethnic (BME) communities such as so-called 'honour-based violence', female genital mutilation (FGM) and forced marriage.

Domestic abuse can include (Home Office, 2010):

- threats of physical violence even though no actual physical force occurs;
- physical violence (such as shoving, hitting, kicking, burning, choking etc.);
- being forced to have sex;
- mental/emotional/psychological cruelty such as name calling, isolation from family and friends, deprivation of family income, being prevented from leaving the home, suffering damage to pets or other personal items;
- using and abusing children in various ways to frighten or force compliance;
- forced marriage;
- FGM and so-called honour-based violence.

In England, Wales and Northern Ireland, domestic violence, domestic abuse and intimate partner violence are terms used interchangeably. In Scotland, the term domestic abuse is preferred, as it is felt this gives a better overall picture of the different aspects that such violence can take. While domestic abuse can be directed at men by women and can happen in same-sex relationships, research shows unequivocally that the majority of domestic abuse (more than 77%) is committed by men against women (Home Office, 2007). Domestic abuse is often a hidden crime, the prevalence and universality of which is well documented (Krug *et al.*, 2002) though it is sometimes difficult to quantify. For instance, although it is generally accepted from UK statistics that one in four women is likely to suffer domestic abuse, we do not have enough reliable knowledge to be more accurate than to say approximately 10% to 50% of women have been physically abused by an intimate male partner (Povey *et al.*, 2008). The British Crime Survey (BCS) states that 45% of women and 26% of men aged 16–59 could recall being subject to an incident of domestic violence (abuse, threats or force), sexual victimisation or stalking at least once in their lifetime (Home Office, 2012). Women are at greater risk of repeat victimisation and serious injury; 89% of those suffering four or more incidents are women (Home Office, 2010). The BCS further reports that half of all women experiencing domestic abuse in the previous year were living with a child under the age of 16 years. However the problem appears slightly greater in Northern Ireland, where the Northern Ireland Crime Survey revealed that almost half (49%) of women with repeat victimisations experienced domestic abuse from a perpetrator on more than one occasion, and that a quarter (27%) were victimised on four or more occasions. For 56% of this group the violence and abuse had started during the perinatal period.

Even if the prevalence of domestic abuse was more widely reported, there is still difficulty in estimating the number of children who have lived with domestic abuse. It cannot be assumed that each victim of domestic abuse is a parent, nor are there any reliable statistics of how many victims are parents. Recently completed research on prevalence of maltreatment of children in the UK found that:

> In all, 3.3 percent of the under 11 year olds and 2.9 percent of the 11 to 17 year olds reported witnessing at least one type of domestic violence in the last twelve months and 12 percent of under 11 year olds, 18.4 percent of 11 to 17 year olds and 24.8 percent of 18 to 24 year olds had witnessed at least one type of parental domestic violence at some time during their childhood (Radford *et al.*, 2011).

Research suggests that the adverse consequences for children decline if they are safe and free from fear of further violence (Hester *et al.*, 2006). Domestic abuse is a major risk factor for child maltreatment, yet studies continue to show that it is both vastly underreported and under-recorded (HMCPSI and HMIC, 2004; Povey *et al.*, 2008).

Children living with and affected by domestic abuse

Within the UK it is estimated that up to one million children have been exposed to domestic abuse (Butchart *et al.*, 2010). Yet, in spite of these stark statistics, there has, until recently, been a systemic failure by public agencies to appreciate that the presence of domestic abuse should be an indicator of the importance of assessing children's need for support and protection if they live in the same household as the victim (Devaney, 2009; Cleaver *et al.*, 2011). Added to this is the fact that children are not included in the definition of domestic abuse and are often the hidden and marginalised victims. However, since 2005, children living in households where domestic abuse is occurring are identified as 'at risk' under the Adoption and Children Act 2002 (HM Government, 2005). Section 120 of this Act has extended the legal definition of harming children to include harm suffered by seeing or hearing ill-treatment of others. Although, system responses are primarily targeted towards adult victims of abuse, recently, increasing attention has been focused on children who witness domestic abuse, as studies estimate that between 10 and 20% of children are at risk for exposure to domestic abuse (Carter and Schechter, 1997; Cawson *et al.*, 2000; Creighton, 2004).

The prevalence data suggests that there are very high numbers of children living with domestic abuse and that it is difficult to protect children from exposure to the effects of some forms of this violence. More recently evidence suggests that one in seven (14.2%) of children and young people under the age of eighteen will have lived with domestic abuse at some point in their childhood (Radford *et al.*, 2011). Children in violent homes may therefore face three risks: the risk of observing traumatic events; the risk of being abused or physically hurt themselves; and the risk of being neglected, both physically and emotionally (Mullender *et al.*, 2003a; Stanley *et al.*, 2011b). A wealth of evidence affirms the notion that few infants and children living with domestic abuse remain unaffected by the experience (Mullender *et al.*, 2003a, 2003b; Osofsky *et al.*, 2004; Humphreys, 2005; Humphreys, 2005; Humphreys *et al.*, 2006; Stanley *et al.*, 2011b), with a UK estimate of one in 20 children, or 750,000 children being exposed every year, witnessing frequent physical violence between parents (Humphreys *et al.*, 2006). Several extensive reviews of published research have found that children who are affected by domestic abuse experience significant negative impacts to the entire range of their well-being and functioning: physical, psychological, emotional, social, behavioural, developmental and cognitive (Carpenter and Stacks 2009; Edleson, 1999; Humphreys *et al.*, 2008; Kitzman *et al.*, 2003; Laing, 2000; McIntosh, 2003; Wolfe *et al.* 2003; Stanley *et al.*, 2011a; Howard *et al.*, 2013).

In addition, the stress of domestic abuse can severely impair women's parenting abilities, making them less able to care for their children and being more depressed than other women (Mian, 2005; Lazenbatt, 2012), factors that can certainly affect their children's well-being (Radford *et al.*, 2006). There is also evidence to suggest that in 75–90% of cases, children are in the same or next room when their mother is being abused (British Medical Association, 1998). Mullender *et al.* (2003a) and Mullender (2004) go as far as saying that in 90% of incidents, infants and children are witnesses to the violence. Infants may be greatly distressed by seeing and hearing the physical and emotional suffering of a parent (Hester *et al.*, 1998; Lundy and Grossman, 2001; Mullender, 2004) and such distress can in itself be psychologically and emotionally harming in the longer term. This can result in infants and children becoming more fearful, anxious, and depressed, having temper-tantrums, sleep disturbances, constantly crying, and having extreme difficulties in nurseries and play school (Hester *et al.*, 2006). The impact of domestic abuse can endure for children long after measures have been taken to ensure their safety (Holt *et al.*, 2008). When infants or children live with domestic abuse experience, they may:

- be in the same room when the incident is taking place;
- hear events as they unfold from another room;
- witness physical damage to an adult or property following an incident;
- be hurt accidentally while trying to intervene;
- be used as a pawn to bargain or threaten with, particularly post separation;
- find themselves used by the abuser in perpetrating violence towards a mother, by using threats or actual violence

towards the child as a way to exert further control;
- witness an undermining of their secure sense of mothering and mother-child relationships;
- become the direct subject of abuse, which may be physical, sexual, or emotional or a combination of these.

And this can affect them in a number of ways that are now very well documented:
- disruptive behaviour;
- difficulties at school;
- physical injury;
- depression, resentment, anger;
- sleep disturbances;
- sense of loss;
- bed wetting and nightmares;
- children as carers;
- guilt, confusion, sadness, self blame;
- fear, anxiety;
- trauma and PTSD;
- loneliness.

Children are very often aware of the domestic abuse even if their mothers believe that they have shielded them from it (Mullender *et al.*, 2002). Children may have lost opportunities and face poorer outcomes because they live with the 'fallout' of domestic abuse and the range of adversities that accompany it – for instance: not being able to bring friends home, missing school, insecure housing, frequently changing addresses. The impact on their well-being can include a range of physical, emotional and behavioural consequences – low self-esteem, depression, PTSD, aggression, running away from home/school and risk-taking behaviour (Hester *et al.*, 2006; Stanley *et al.*, 2011a). One systematic review concluded that while the association between domestic abuse, harm to children's health and use of health services is not straightforward, known adverse consequences include heightened risks of under immunisation and of risk-taking behaviour in adolescence (Bair-Merritt *et al.*, 2006).

There are however a range of protective factors that can influence the extent of the impact of domestic abuse, including in particular the relationship with a familiar and caring adult (usually the mother)

(Holt *et al.*, 2008). A study with 8–16 year olds cited mothers as 'their most important source of help than anyone in their lives' (Mullender *et al.*, 2002). Gorin's (2004) review of children's experiences of domestic violence found four main types of coping strategies:

- avoidance/distraction (e.g. finding somewhere to go, a 'haven', hiding, blocking it out, turning up the TV);
- protection/inaction (e.g. keeping watch, staying awake at night);
- confrontation, intervening and self destruction; and
- positive action and help seeking.

Children may not want to talk about their problems at the time. Some fear the abuser's reaction if they tell, or if the police become involved. They worry they may not be believed. Boys are less likely to talk and this is confirmed from experiences in ChildLine. Children rarely go to professional services as the first port of call for support and are most likely to turn to informal sources, friends, siblings or family. Rigorous research into how adult interventions impact on the child, from the child's point of view, is limited, with some recent projects attempting to correct the gap (Galvani, 2010). For example, the NSPCC are evaluating a number of programmes that were developed originally for adults, and are evaluating the impact these have on children's well-being (Galvani, 2010; McConnell *et al.*, in press; McManus *et al.*, 2013).

Not only children but also teenagers and young girls suffering teen relationship abuse experience greater incidence rates, more frequent sexual violence and severe abuse, and suffer more negative impacts including higher levels of coercive control, compared with boys (Barter *et al.*, 2009; Barter and McCarry, 2012). Therefore the consequences of domestic abuse for all ages of children is immense, as children may be experiencing life in poverty, or homelessness, and becoming involved in youth offending or teenage pregnancy. Sexual and emotional abuse is also more likely to happen within these families (Royal College of Psychiatrists, 2011b). Even without direct abuse, the devastating physical and emotional effect of domestic abuse on children and young people severely affects their sense of safety, their mental health and well-being, achievement and development, despite the best efforts of the non-abusing parent to protect them (Royal College of Psychiatrists, 2011c; Royal College of Psychiatry and Child Health, 2004).

HIGH RISK FAMILIES
Co-occurrence of domestic and child abuse

It is not only the exposure of living with domestic abuse that creates vulnerability in children and young people. It is now widely accepted that children living with domestic abuse experience are also at greater risk of experiencing neglect, physical and/or sexual abuse, as there is strong evidence to indicate that child abuse and exposure to domestic abuse often co-occur (Dong *et al.*, 2004; Sousa *et al.*, 2011). Children living with domestic abuse are also more likely to be directly physically or sexually abused. In the US child maltreatment has been reported to be a risk marker of domestic abuse with each year seeing an estimated 3.3 million children exposed to family violence and abuse (Thornberry *et al.*, 2012). Numerous studies report on this problematic co-occurrence. A meta-analysis by Edleson (1999) of thirty-one high quality research studies showed that between 30% and 66% of children who endure physical abuse are also living in a context of domestic abuse. The variation is largely dependent on research site and methodology, but either figure is disturbing. The severity of violence is also relevant. Romito *et al.*, (2005), for example, found that in a US study of 3,363 parents there was an almost 100% correlation between the most severe abuse of women and the men's physical abuse of children. An association of between 45% and 70% has been found between a father's violence to the mother and his violence to the children (Goodall and Lumley, 2007). We also know that the rates of child abuse and neglect are fifteen times higher than the national average where domestic abuse is an issue; indeed in three out of five cases of maltreatment, domestic abuse is also an issue. Studies show that the more severe the violence, the greater the risk of children being physically abused (Edleson, 2001). Prolonged and/or regular exposure to domestic abuse can, despite the best efforts of the parents to protect the child, seriously affect an infant's psychosocial development, health and emotional well-being in a number of ways in both the short and longer terms. In the last national prevalence study, 26% of children and young people reported physical violence during their childhood (Cawson *et al.*, 2000). This does not seem to have changed over time, with the most recent prevalence study showing that a quarter of children who live with domestic abuse experience are physically abused themselves (Radford *et al.*, 2011). Furthermore, almost three-quarters of children on the 'at risk' register live in households where domestic abuse occurs (Mullender *et al.*, 2003a; Lewis and Drife, 2007).

Domestically abused mothers

Not only is there a link between domestic abuse and maltreatment, but abuse can impact detrimentally on parenting abilities; it jeopardises the developmental progress and personal abilities of children and young people, contributing to cycles of adversity; and it disrupts broader family functioning and the home environment (Buckley *et al.*, 2007). Very often, public and professional people may blame the mother, for not nurturing the child as she should, for staying in a violent relationship and for allowing contact between the child and the perpetrator. But one study of 200 women with domestic abuse experiences showed that 60% had left the family home because they were afraid the perpetrator would kill the child (Humphreys *et al.*, 2002). Co-occurring depression and PTSD, which have substantial co-morbidity, are the most prevalent mental-health sequelae of domestic abuse, with low self-esteem and feelings of inferiority heightening the risk of re-victimisation (Meltzer *et al.*, 2009). Systematic reviews and meta-analyses show that the negative mental-health consequences of domestic abuse and symptoms of PTSD and other psychological stress reactions are long-term both for mothers and their children (Howard *et al.*, 2010; Trevillion *et al.*, 2012). Abused women are three times more likely to be diagnosed with mental illness and three times more likely to report depression (Trevillion *et al.*, 2012), five times more likely to attempt suicide (Pico-Alfonso *et al.*, 2005) nine times more likely to misuse drugs (Dutton, 1992; Coker *et al.*, 2002), and fifteen times more likely to misuse alcohol (Beaulaurier *et al.*, 2007). Homelessness is also a major problem for abused women but especially so for black and Asian women as housing acceptances are often due to domestic abuse (Women and Equality Unit, 2003). Importantly Anooshian's (2005) review of homeless children highlights that exposure to domestic abuse was seen as a consequence of homelessness as well as a cause. The impact of living with the abuse may be compounded by the woman's coping responses which in many cases may be negative, with mothers using alcohol or drugs to manage the relationship difficulties. Such negative coping strategies can lead to women suffering from mental-health disorders such as depression and anxiety (Mezey *et al.*, 2005).

Child homicide

In spite of the best efforts of those working within the child-protection system, child deaths as a result of abuse and neglect remain a serious problem across all four nations in the UK (UNICEF, 2003). Child homicide is also now increasingly seen within a context of domestic abuse. For example, children who have been killed by their fathers or step-fathers were also living with domestic abuse, as evidenced in high profile cases (Radford *et al.*, 2006). Cavanagh *et al.* (2007) reviewed twenty-six child deaths, finding that nearly two-thirds were murdered by fathers or step-fathers who also abused the child's mother. The latest bi-annual analysis of serious case reviews (SCRs) in England conducted an intensive assessment of forty children's cases and found that in 21 of these the children had lived with or where currently living with domestic abuse at the time of their serious injury or death (Brandon and Thoburn, 2008). However, previously in a review of forty SCRs conducted between 2001 and 2003 Rose and Barnes (2008) highlighted the lack of significance attributed to domestic violence and the impact this may have been having on the child or children of the family, despite the presence of violence in the home being well known to a number of agencies. In similar vein, an Ofsted (Ofsted, 2011b) report showed variation in police practice in terms of the recording of incidents of domestic violence and in identifying children at risk.

These findings are mirrored in Northern Ireland where Case Management Reviews highlight some of the factors which contributed to parents' inability to assure their children's safety and well-being such as living with domestic violence (Devaney *et al.*, 2011). Lack of recognition of the risks posed by domestic violence and sexually harmful behaviour were noted in two Northern Ireland cases.

Importantly, child contact visits with a parent who is a domestic violence perpetrator are frequently flashpoints for further violence and harassment (Radford *et al.*, 2011). A review of child homicides found that in a five year period twenty-nine children were killed in the context of post separation contact visits (Sanders, 2006). Domestic abuse is also associated with maternal and foetal deaths (CEMACH, 2004), for some violence starts or becomes more severe in pregnancy or shortly after birth (McCosker-Howard and Woods, 2006).

Perinatal period as a high risk period

Pregnancy is identified as a 'high risk' period for domestic abuse, prompting the initial episode, or an escalation of a pre-existing abusive relationship (Stewart and Cecutti, 1993; Scobie and McGuire, 1999; Sidebotham and Golding, 2001; Shadigian and Bauer, 2004; Lazenbatt, 2010). Evidence suggest that more than 30% of domestic abuse begins in pregnancy (Bacchus and Bewley 2002; Lewis and Drife 2007) and prevalence rates range from 1% to 20% depending on the definition of violence in the study, although most studies report prevalence rates between 3% and 16% (Gazmararian *et al.*, 1996; Gazmararian, 2000; Jasinski, 2004). Although domestic abuse crosses all cultural and social divides, findings from a review by Jasinski (2004) highlight several factors associated with pregnancy-related abuse such as: poverty; low socio-economic status; low levels of social support; teenage and first-time parenting; unexpected or unwanted pregnancy; ethnicity; and drug and alcohol abuse. Domestic abuse during pregnancy and the first six months of child rearing is significantly related to various types of child maltreatment (child physical abuse, neglect, and emotional abuse) up to the child's fifth year, with infants under one year at the highest risk of injury or death (Kotch *et al.*, 1999; McGuigan and Pratt, 2001; Butchart and Villaveces, 2003; Goodall and Lumley 2007). A recent review by Howard *et al.*, (2013) provides evidence to suggest that there is a significant relationship between high levels of perinatal anxiety, depression, and PTSD and the experience of pregnancy-related domestic abuse. Research is now needed to assess and evaluate how maternity and mental-health services can work together more effectively to address the consequences of domestic abuse and improve perinatal outcomes for mothers and their infants.

Although a causal relationship between exposure to violence during pregnancy and adverse perinatal outcomes has not been clearly demonstrated, pregnant women who experience domestic abuse are more likely than non-abused women to have conditions that place their unborn child at serious risk (Hunt and Martin 2001). Domestic abuse also poses a serious risk even to the unborn foetus, as violence may increase the risk of antepartum haemorrhage, urinary tract infections, premature birth and low birth weight, placental damage (a prime cause of miscarriage or stillbirth), chorioamnionitis, foetal injury and in the worse cases, death (Mezey and Bewley, 1997; Bacchus and Bewley, 2002). Violence against pregnant women has been referred to as 'child abuse in the womb' (Mirrlees-Black, 1999). There has been concern for some time, particularly in the US, about the issue of 'foetal abuse', where a foetus may be damaged *in utero* by acts of omission or commission (Mezey and Bewley, 1997). Importantly, foetal morbidity from violence is more prevalent than that from gestational diabetes or preeclampsia (Osofsky, 2003) and can have detrimental effects on the developing infant's brain (Sidebotham and Fleming, 2007).

This co-occurrence of risk factors for violence in pregnancy, where the health and safety of two potential victims is placed in jeopardy (Mezey *et al.*, 2003; 2005; Lazenbatt *et al.*, 2009) stresses the importance for health professionals such as midwives, health visitors and GPs to be able to recognise and report domestic and/or child abuse at this time. However, assessing domestic abuse as a child-protection issue has been relatively slow in gaining health professional acceptance, even though the international evidence suggests that there is a clear and irrefutable link between domestic abuse and the co-occurrence of child abuse (Edleson, 1999; Shipman *et al.*, 1999; McGuigan and Pratt, 2001; Hartley, 2002; 2004; Osofsky, 2003; Lundy and Grossman, 2001). Similarly, Edleson's (1999) review of 321 studies on the overlap of domestic abuse and child maltreatment found co-occurrence rates between 30% and 60% in the majority of studies reviewed. Using more conservative criteria for defining child abuse, Appel and Holden (1998) reviewed a similar set of studies and identified a co-occurrence rate of 40%, while a study in Ireland shows that 52% of both domestic and child abuse cases are inflicted by the same perpetrator (MacIntyre and Carr, 1999). There is also increasing evidence of the co-occurrence of domestic abuse and child sexual abuse, and of rape and sexual assault with domestic abuse (Mullender *et al.*, 2003b; Walby and Allen, 2004).

EFFECTIVE INTERVENTION

To understand what types of interventions might work for children and their families, we need to understand better the underlying cause. There are three main theories of domestic abuse perpetration:

Feminist theory – the most commonly cited theory of domestic abuse in which male battering is attributed to a patriarchal society (Dobash and Dobash, 1992; Bagshaw *et al.*, 2000; Pence and Paymer, 1993).

Social learning theory – where violence in the home is a learnt behaviour where perpetrators see other family members or friends being aggressive and obtaining positive results from their aggression (Bandura, 1977; Pence and Paymer 1993).

Individual/familial theory – where other explanations such as per-sonality disorders and emotional problems are used as reasons why domestic abuse is perpetrated. This also includes family systems theo-ries where all members of the family contribute to the violence (Mau-ricio and Gormley, 2001).

Feminist theory, however, does not explain adequately why some men are perpetrators and others are not. Neither do all men who grow up in violent households go on to become perpetrators of domestic abuse. Thus social learning theory is not fully applicable. Individual and family systems theories are criticised for ignoring power dynamics in families and not assigning blame, which can put safety of victims and children at risk. Each theory of domes-tic abuse has an associated intervention, although recent trends show that models are being developed to address perpetrators as a heterogeneous group. The Duluth model is the widest used and also the most controversial, with other programmes often based on aspects of Duluth, in particular the accredited programmes offered by *Respect*.

While there is a variety of perpetrator programmes, few have been rigorously evaluated to show that they are effective. A systematic review of cognitive behavioural therapy interventions found only six trials, mostly in the US, but effect sizes so small and confidence intervals so wide there was no clear evidence of effect (Smedslund *et al.*, 2011). Many perpetrator programmes have been created by researchers and practitioners with extensive experience in domestic abuse, but different methods are recommended, based on the theory used by the developers. Systematic reviewers question whether one specific method is appropriate and if programmes should be offered to meet the needs of the specific individual, because perpetrators are not a homogenous group. The one programme that comes closest to tailoring the intervention provided to the perpetrator's particular needs is that developed by *Respect*. A multisite, rigorous evaluation of the *Respect* programme is being undertaken, but this evaluation is not yet completed and conclusions about effectiveness would be premature (Westmarland *et al.*, 2010).

PARENTAL MENTAL HEALTH CHALLENGES

Approximately one in six adults in Britain has been diagnosed with a neurotic disorder such as depression, anxiety or phobias (Office for National Statistics, 2001). In addition, approximately five in 1000 people surveyed were assessed as having a severe mental disorder such as schizophrenia or bipolar depression. It is hard to capture the effects of mental illness as it may vary and be perceived differently from case to case.

According to Tunnard's review (2004), parents with mental-health problems have a high risk of living in poverty and in isolation and there are also low employment rates among people with mental illness. There are also links between mental illness and domestic abuse and substance misuse (Stanley *et al.*, 2003; Cleaver *et al.*, 2011). There is evidence to show that relationships between parents can become strained (Tunnard, 2004), although this does not mean that they have a poor relationship with their children. Various studies have looked at the effects of parental mental-health illness on children. It has been found that many children living with parental mental illness take a caring role (Aldridge, 2006) and that the responsibilities undertaken by children can vary depending on the parent's illness.

In a study to explore the impact of parental mental health on children (Stallard *et al.*, 2004), half of the parents interviewed said they felt their children did not understand their illness, whereas 11 of 26 children said they felt that no one explained their parent's mental illness properly and they were continuously not being informed. This can be distressing particularly in cases where stressful situations emerge, such as when parents overdose or are emotionally volatile. In addition, it was found that professionals working with the parents can overlook children's needs, including keeping the children informed of their parent's condition, even if the child is a carer.

Studies have shown some of the negative effects for children who have parents with mental illness (Stallard *et al.*, 2004; Aldridge, 2006; Tunnard, 2004). These may include restrictions on social life and friendships, lack of confidence and low self-esteem, prone to being bullied, restricted life choices, developing mental-health problems, depression, eating disorders, overdosing, self-harm, stress, emotional distress, behavioural disturbances, missing school, educational difficulties and lack of educational attainment, inappropriate sexual behaviour, obsessive-compulsive behaviour, aggressive outbursts and delinquency. In addition, there have been studies that have linked parental mental illness to child abuse. In a Canadian study, Walsh *et al.*, (2002) interviewed 8548 respondents on parental psychiatric history. They found that there was a two to three-fold increase in the prevalence of child abuse if the parents had depression, mania and schizophrenia. Measures to support families are therefore crucial. Smith (2004) found similar results in her review of the impact of parental mental illness on children. Smith discusses how the characteristics of certain mental illness can result in physical and emotional injuries or neglect if a child is present when these symptoms are manifesting themselves. For example, high levels of irritability in mothers suffering from depression when regarding their child. Smith also found evidence to suggest that mothers with poor mental health have a higher incidence of physically punishing their child. It is important to note, however, that most research either looks at parental mental illness from the mother's or parent's perspective, and although there are some studies addressing fathers, they are few and far between.

Leverton's review (2003) of psychiatric studies on the impact of each type of parental mental illness on children found evidence to suggest that children living with parents with panic disorders had an increased risk of also having panic disorders themselves and agoraphobia. She found that many studies suggested children living with parents with bipolar depression had higher levels of mood disorder and higher rates of attention and behavioural problems. There are very limited studies exploring the impact of different types of parental mental illness on children.

Services need to be defragmented so as to work with each family member in order to make the family work as a whole (Gladstone *et al.*, 2006; Statham, 2004). There is also strong evidence to suggest that family therapy can be as effective, if not more effective, than individual therapies and medication (Carr, 2009). Although the results of studies in Carr's review are still limited, they provide a platform for future research into alternative therapies to that of individual therapy and medication. Although most studies discuss parental mental health, it is likely that by parents they mean mothers (Daniel and Taylor, 2001) and the gendered aspects require more unpacking.

PARENTAL SUBSTANCE MISUSE

Substance misuse by parents is a significant risk factor for children, but very often there is little differentiation between drugs and alcohol. We argue that separating these is important, as interventions need to be managed differently. Drug use, for example, can be controlled to time and place and having supportive partners or family around. Alcohol may result in more volatility and violence and unpredictability.

Approximately 30% of children under 16 years of age live with at least one binge-drinking parent (Manning *et al.*, 2009). An analysis of 230 call records to ChildLine Scotland showed that the most common problem children called about was physical abuse (2/5 of children), much of which was while under the influence of alcohol. While this represents a significant problem, much of the research has not disaggregated drugs and alcohol. Galvani (2004) interviewed 19 UK women who were victims of domestic abuse on their views of the role of alcohol on their partner's behaviour. She found that although most women found alcohol acted as a disinhibitor for aggressive behaviour, violence and abuse usually happened as a result of other factors in addition to the alcohol consumption. Alcohol acted as a lubricant for these situations but was not the sole cause of violence and abuse. Alcohol misuse can affect key aspects of family life such as roles, rituals, routines, social life, finances, communication and conflict (Velleman, 1993). Multidisciplinary family services that address the issues around alcohol and also work with the family together and individually have shown some effect for families who stick to the programme (Velleman *et al.*, 2003).

It is estimated that between 200,000 and 300,000 children in England and Wales and between 41,000 and 59,000 children in Scotland have one or both parents with a serious drug problem (Advisory Council on the Misuse of Drugs, 2003; Advisory Council on the Misuse of Drugs, 2007). Although there is very limited data on Northern Ireland, it is anticipated that around 40,000 children live with parents who misuse alcohol or other substances (Department of Health Social Services and Public Safety, 2009). Substance misuse is increasingly being regarded as one of the most problematic and challenging areas to tackle in the area of child abuse and child protection and accounts for the overwhelming majority of cases that remain open and/or are re-referred to social services (Forrester, 2007). Services and measures in place are either therefore insufficient or inadequate in tackling this problem. Not enough research has been done within the UK on substance misuse and its link to child protection and interventions (Montgomery *et al.*, 2009). However, the increasing majority of studies undertaken in the UK have suggested that although substance misuse is prevalent in cases of domestic abuse and child protection, this issue is either not being addressed or even being recorded as a cause for concern (Humphreys 2005; Forrester, 2000).

Drug misuse can manifest itself in a variety of ways which include physical ailments such as infections, overdoses and accidental and non-accidental injuries and psychological impairments such as being dominated by the drug and addiction, withdrawal symptoms such as erratic and irritable behaviour, psychosis and serious memory lapses (Advisory Council on the Misuse of Drugs, 2003). Such symptoms suggest it is likely that children living with parents who engage in drug misuse are at high risk of significant harm. However, most people who have interacted with drugs do not suffer these long lasting effects. In fact reviews tell us that there is little evidence to suggest that substance misuse alone is a risk factor (Templeton *et al.*, 2006). Rather it is intertwined with other personal, cultural and societal factors (Kroll, 2004. Whittaker and Elliott's study of drug-abusing men in Scotland (Whittaker and Elliott, 2010) demonstrated a commitment to 'good' fatherhood and attempts by the men to do the best they could for their children. Negative manifestations usually start emerging when there is a combination of other factors such as mental state, physiological impact of the substance, expectations of the individual regarding oneself and others, personality, type, dosage and method of administration.

Forrester (2000) explored the correlation between drugs and alcohol and abuse. He looked at fifty families on the Child Protection Register in the inner London area, and assessed to what extent substance misuse was present and whether it was noted as an issue. He found that alcohol misuse was present in 28 of the families and it had the strongest correlation with neglect. However, there were also cases of emotional and physical abuse in families where alcohol misuse was recorded. In a later study in London (Forrester, 2007) substance misuse, especially alcohol, was strongly linked to violence. Many services working with domestic abuse also note a prevalence of substance misuse by perpetrators and survivors (Humphreys, 2005; Velleman, 1993; Kroll, 2004, 2007; Kroll and Taylor 2003; Velleman and Orford 1999; Cleaver *et al.*, 2011).

In cases where substance misuse is having detrimental effects, these effects can also impact on the substance user's family. Bancroft and Wilson (Bancroft and Wilson 2007) interviewed 15–27 year olds who lived with parental substance misuse. They found that the impact of parental substance misuse on children may vary. They argue that by having a risk gradient (as suggested in

Hidden Harm) one could overlook the needs children and young people want and need to be addressed. Effects may include lack of care, neglect, growing up in an unstable and violent environment, criminality, lack of or hindered education and developmental and health problems. Not all people who use or misuse substances will be abusive or bad parents. Again, there is usually a combination of factors that may lead to one having aggressive and abusive behaviour. A significant proportion of the literature regarding the impact of parental substance misuse on children has started focusing on resilience (Templeton, 2006; Bancroft and Wilson 2007).

Certain psychotherapeutic approaches can be effective in producing optimal parenting with heroin addicted mothers (Barlow and Schrader-MacMillan 2009; Barnard and McKeganey, 2002; Copello *et al.*, 2006). Intensive family interventions that support families in times of crisis, helps the substance misuser to identify their drug/alcohol issues and help them change, and help keep families together and moreover safe have shown very promising results (Forrester and Williams, 2010; Woolfall *et al.*, 2008). However, long-term sustainability is often difficult to maintain. Services that aim to improve communication between parent and child and help them understand addiction have been found to be successful (Zohhadi *et al.*, 2006).

There remains a gap however between children's and adult services (Kennedy, 2010). In a study that explored children's and families' experiences of social care in child-protection cases, Cleaver *et al.*, (2006) found that although there were many cases of co-morbidity, services would tend to identify the needs of one of the family members as opposed to all. In addition, it was found that in cases of co-morbidity within child protection, social services case files suggest that there was very low collaboration between specialist agencies and that interventions were more successful when families had only one issue, for example domestic abuse, and not various issues such as substance misuse and domestic abuse. Further research is needed into the role of fathers and their impact, as well as into resilience (Templeton *et al.*, 2006).

Interventions for substance and alcohol misuse

Inter-agency/Multidisciplinary work – Not enough work is being done in this area. As a result, certain needs are being addressed over others when a comprehensive approach is necessary. The most important intervention needs to be a holistic one where different agencies work together to produce an all-encompassing and moreover effective intervention.

More child-oriented research and services – Not enough research has been done on this topic in terms of what works. In addition, more research needs to be undertaken in terms of what children need and want from services.

Inter-agency awareness-raising and training – Services that do not specialise in issues of substance misuse, but work with this area, need to be trained and made aware of the services and options available, as well as how to work with these cases.

Further research into resilience and coping – Resilience and coping have shown to be potentially effective for increasing the life chances of children and young people living with parental substance misuse.

More feminist research – Studies have shown that there may be significant differences in the impact of paternal and maternal substance misuse when coupled with the different roles each parent has within the family.

Family Alcohol Services – Have been effective at bridging the gap between addressing alcohol misuse and the needs of the family.

Option two and Family First Model –Have generated very positive results with families in crisis and if coupled with longer-term support services, this could be an effective tool in tackling parental substance misuse and associated problems.

Parent and Child Together – Not only works with the issue of substance misuse but also with the breakdown in communication and family relationships.

Coping Skills Training – There is a strong link between violence and substance and this approach has shown that it not only reduces substance misuse but also violence towards oneself and others.

Updated guidance from the Scottish Government (2013) emphasises not only the importance of multi-agency working to deliver a coordinated response by services, but the expectations on strategic leaders and local planning services to support that response and operational delivery of services. These may need to be beyond the substance misuse issue.

TEENAGE PARENTS

Much attention has been given to associations between teenage pregnancy and negative outcomes: child abuse and neglect (Burghes and Brown, 1995), poor parenting (Kotagal, 1993), high stress levels, school dropout, limited educational opportunities (Furstenberg *et al.*, 1987), as well as multiple pregnancies at a young age (Britner and Reppucci, 1997). In addition, children living with single parents and stepfamilies are at greater risk than other families of physical abuse (O'Connor, 2002) and have poorer school performance. Unfortunately, there is a lack of national statistical data on the neglect and abuse perpetrated by teenage parents and incidence is projected only from research samples.

A systematic review (Black *et al.*, 2001) on the issue had mixed results, although overall there was found to be a moderate association between younger age and minor physical aggression, particularly in mothers (Straus *et al.*, 1990; Straus *et al.*, 1998; Connelly and Straus, 1992). Young mothers are perhaps more prone to suffer from depression and are less emotionally available to their child than older mothers (Osofsky, 1993). Due to their immaturity and limited knowledge and experience, their parenting skills are seen to be limited and therefore of poorer quality (Moore and Rosenthal 1993). Teenage parents are more likely to '*resort to inappropriate child-rearing techniques as a result of impatience, substance abuse, frustration and stress*' (Herrenkohl *et al.*, 1998).

There are however, studies that challenge all these views. For instance Phoenix (1991) demonstrates that despite young mothers often facing particularly difficult economic hardship, they are nonetheless determined to do the best for their child just as well as older mothers living in similar circumstances. Vary (2000) provides evidence that young parents, particularly mothers, take the responsibilities of parenthood very seriously and that the needs of the children are put on a high agenda, even to the detriment of the parents' own physical and emotional needs. In a secondary analysis of data from the longitudinal Children of the 90s Study investigating the impact of teenage motherhood on children (Golding, 2004), the children of teenage mothers did not appear to be any worse off than the children of older mothers on many developmental outcomes.

However, corroborating findings in the *British Cohort Study, 1970* (Parsons *et al.*, 2012) found adolescent motherhood played a role in the transmission of social disadvantage. (Since BCS70 began, there have been eight full data collection exercises in order to monitor the cohort members' health, education, social and economic circumstances.) The BCS70 investigation found that both mothers and children faced adverse outcomes in terms of their mental health and behavioural adjustment, respectively (Berrington *et al.*, 2005; Parsons *et al.*, 2012).There are limitations to be considered with the data that is available on teenage parenting and child abuse. We have gained much insight into the importance of the issue and the correlates of teen pregnancy, but little outcome evaluation exists for maltreatment prevention programmes in general (Dubowitz, 1990; Fink and McCloskey, 1990), including parent education and support programmes designed to address teen parents in particular (Altepeter and Walker, 1992). Hence, mostly data is centred on the relationship around vulnerable adolescents and the relationship with their parents where pregnancy is an outcome. Although effective interventions to reduce the occurrence of teenage pregnancies have been identified (Manlove and Child Trends Incorporated, 2002; Manlove *et al.*, 2004), there is limited data on teen parents and the possible implications on their children. Most interventions focus on the mother. To date, there has been little systematic evaluation on child focused-interventions particularly in the area of child abuse (Montgomery *et al.*, 2009).

There appears to be more emphasis on parent-focused interventions, to help improve their parenting skills and parent-child interactions. If effective, there is an assumption that this will help prevent recurrence of abuse as well as reduce parent–child conflict and coercive interaction (Carr, 2009). Although there is a relatively limited evidence base on this, often these interventions are used in practice with families presenting multiple problems including child maltreatment (Montgomery *et al.*, 2009). While family-focused preventative interventions may appear to be beneficial by involving parent or caregiver, there appears to be little promising outcome (Montgomery *et al.*, 2009). Engaging teenage parents on such programmes is also difficult. Moreover, while there is substantial data on physical abuse committed by single teenage mothers, there is very little on fathers, making it difficult to understand the extent of perpetration by both parents.

FOETAL ALCOHOL HARM

Foetal alcohol harm has been, and continues to be, given different names in different countries by different groups. In part, this is because it is difficult to diagnose. Foetal Alcohol Syndrome (FAS) is the most widely recognised and agreed clinical diagnosis – for which there are four internationally recognised diagnostic criteria. However, researchers and practitioners are largely in agreement that full-blown FAS is only the proverbial 'tip of the iceberg' of the spectrum of foetal alcohol harm (Sher, 2010). FAS occurs from Teratogenic effects early in the pregnancy, when facial features and internal organs are at a crucial stage in their development. Brain damage from alcohol exposure can occur at any time during pregnancy. Prenatal exposure to alcohol is the leading cause of brain damage and development delay among children in industrial countries. Although invisible, this alcohol harm eventually shows up in learning disabilities and behavioural problems.

The most common impact is on the brain's so-called 'executive functions', that is, the ability to: plan, learn from experience and control impulses. The 'hooks' within the brain on which to hang these executive functions are often diminished to some extent and can be largely missing (Sher, 2010). There is no test before or during pregnancy that can predict the level of risk or the birth outcome for a particular woman. Alcohol can cause a miscarriage or stillbirth, as well as birth defects. There is no 100% safe time to drink an absolutely safe amount of alcohol. The only certainty is that no alcohol from conception until birth always results in no foetal alcohol harm.

Sher (2010) likens it to the visual impairment spectrum. Everyone needing corrective spectacles is a part of this spectrum, but only a relatively small number are blind. And yet, with foetal alcohol harm, the spectrum is much less about degree of severity and much more about the difficulty of distinguishing it from other conditions having similar effects. And, of course, some people suffer from both foetal harm and other problems simultaneously – a reality that makes diagnosis and treatment complex (Golden, 2005). Foetal alcohol harm is potentially 100% preventable by abstaining from consuming alcohol during the entire pregnancy, but is nonetheless only potentially preventable because abstinence may be impossible for women with a serious alcohol problem. In these cases, contraception may be a better option. Drinking during pregnancy is better understood as potentially having a lifelong negative impact on the well-being and life chances of the baby.

In 2013 the first international conference on the prevention of FAS was held in Toronto, Canada. This conference resulted in the production and endorsement of an international charter, signed by senior representatives from more than thirty-five countries, which was seen as an urgent call for action (Jonsson *et al.*, 2014). The charter emphasised the responsibility of both men and women and that governments need to promote a consistent and evidence-based message about prevention: to abstain from alcohol use during pregnancy is the only certain way to prevent FAS disorder.

OTHER RISK FACTORS

A systematic review of the correlates of child neglect (Connell-Carrick, 2003) has identified a variety of child, parent and environmental characteristics that are associated with an increased risk of maltreatment. Connell-Carrick's review also offers some comparison with the risk factors involved in physical abuse. Parents who physically abuse tend to be younger and are most often the birthparent, usually the mother. They also have mental-health symptomatology including low self-esteem, depression, social isolation and loneliness. Physically abusive parents tend to be more hostile and aggressive with their children than neglectful parents and tend to have high expectations of their child's behaviour, which can result in a physically punitive occurrence when the child does not meet parental expectation (Connell-Carrick, 2003). Both neglecting and physically abusive parents tend to view their children as temperamentally difficult. Although families who neglect and families who physically abuse their children both tend to come from economically disadvantaged backgrounds, the risk of neglect in families with low incomes is greater than that of physical abuse. While victims of neglect do not tend to be of a certain gender victims of child physical abuse are more often male than female. Although child disability is correlated with both physical abuse and neglect, the incidence of physical abuse is higher in children with disabilities than children who are neglected.

Conclusion

This chapter set out the case for concentrating on high risk families. There is a particular focus on domestic abuse, often occurring concurrently with child abuse, compromising parenting abilities and sometimes resulting in child homicide. The perinatal period is a time of particular vulnerability to domestic abuse. Effective interventions rely on understanding underlying causes, but current theoretical positioning remains incomplete.

Parental mental ill health varies case to case and person to person, but parents with mental-health problems often have a higher risk of unemployment and subsequent poverty and isolation. There are also links with domestic abuse and with misuse of substances, and sometimes these factors can be problematic for a child's development and safety.

Use of drugs and alcohol by parents can likewise provide an unhealthy milieu for growing up, affecting the parenting environment and potentially exposing children to dangerous behaviours and risky individuals. Interventions that work with children and parents are crucial.

Finally, we examined the evidence around some of the other risk factors for child maltreatment in high risk families, including teenage parenting and foetal alcohol harm. In the following chapter we unpack what is mean by violence for children, and the effects this has on them.

CHAPTER 2

Understanding violence and the effects of violence

Introduction

As stated in the previous chapter, child maltreatment is one of the most serious events undermining healthy psychological well-being and development, and no other social risk factor has a stronger association with developmental psychopathology (Osofsky and Lieberman, 2011).

Child abuse or neglect and general trauma, including witnessing violence, alter normal child development and, without intervention, can have lifelong consequences (Scannapieco and Connell-Carrick, 2005).

This chapter discusses the physical and psychological effects of different forms of maltreatment and shows how the consequences of child abuse are serious and significant: for the individual; for society as a whole; and potentially for future generations. It provides evidence that infancy is a window of opportunity for preventative interventions and a crucial time to reduce later developmental difficulties, and encourage stronger infant–parent relationships. Controversial issues such as 'Shaken Baby Syndrome', 'Female genital mutilation/cutting', 'Filicide', Fabricated and Induced Illness (FII) are all debated and the consequences highlighted for children and families.

The effects of this violence show that an average of twenty-three children under one are killed each year in the UK (Scottish Government, 2010; Smith, 2011; Police Service of Northern Ireland, 2011) and data from Serious Case Reviews (SCRs) in England and Wales consistently highlight that close to 50% of all maltreatment-related deaths and serious injuries involve infants under one, with a substantial proportion being of babies of three months or younger (Department of Education, 2010). Parents are almost always the perpetrators, with infants being eight times more likely to be killed than older children (Smith, 2011). However, this may only be the 'tip of the iceberg', and it is suggested that well over 50% of fatalities due to maltreatment may be incorrectly coded as deaths due to accidents, natural causes or other factors on the death record (Putnam-Hornstein *et al.*, 2011).

Infants are an especially vulnerable group to the effects of violence, as international and UK evidence consistently shows that infants under one are more at risk of fatal injury, physical abuse and neglect than any other age group (Smith, 2011; Sidebotham and Fleming, 2007), mainly because they are almost completely dependent on others for their overall well-being and development and, ultimately, their survival. Infants who are exposed to one type of maltreatment are often exposed to other types on several occasions or continuously (Finkelhor and Ormrod, 2010; Finkelhor *et al.*, 2013). How frequently this abuse occurs is underestimated by official reports because recording of more than one type of maltreatment is often discouraged by child-protection agencies, and official reports often do not capture the chronology of exposure over time. Infants and young children who have suffered several types of maltreatment are significantly more likely to have special educational needs or a long-standing disability or illness; and likely to have a parent with enduring physical, learning or mental-health problems, or drug and/or alcohol misuse (Finkelhor, 2008; Finkelhor *et al.*, 2013). Such children have often experienced other forms of child maltreatment as well, including emotional abuse, neglect, physical abuse and witnessing domestic abuse in the home (Radford *et al.*, 2006; Finkelhor *et al.*, 2013). The following sections will highlight the effects of violence on infants and children. To begin, the following section will examine one of the most common causes of infant death or long-term disability from child abuse, namely, non-accidental head injury (NAHI). Sidebotham and Fleming (2007) describe this as a severe form of abuse, with 13–30% mortality rates, while Dias *et al.* (2005) report significant neurological impairments in at least half of the survivors.

NON-ACCIDENTAL HEAD INJURY AND SHAKEN BABY SYNDROME

Infants and young children aged from birth to five years have disproportionately high rates of maltreatment (Osofsky and Lieberman, 2011) as they are more vulnerable to all forms of abuse, especially neglect and physical abuse. This group makes up a significant proportion of child-protection registrations (CPR) across the UK, accounting for 13% of children subject to a child protection plan in England, 12.5% of children on the CPR in Wales and 7% of children on the CPR in Northern Ireland in 2008/09 (Bunting, 2011).

Comparison of parental reports of physical and emotional cruelty towards children under three with reports to child-protection agencies has also revealed maltreatment rates in the general population may be up to twenty-five times higher than child-protection statistics would indicate (Sidebotham and Golding, 2001).

Infant maltreatment is, therefore, one of the most serious events undermining healthy psychological development, and no other social risk factor has a stronger association with developmental psychopathology (Belsky *et al.*, 2010). Abusive head injury (known as NAHI in infants) is the primary injury mechanism by which physically maltreated infants sustain serious and often fatal injuries. US research has also shown that young children who developed a cerebral infarct after being admitted to hospital for closed head injury were six times more likely to have been abused than patients without infarcts (Ransom *et al.*, 2003). NICE (2009) guidelines indicate that abusive head injury with associated intracranial injury, while relatively uncommon in the overall population, is much more prevalent among infants than other ages groups, with an estimated incidence of 35 per 100,000 children younger than six months, 14–21 per 100,000 children under one and 0.3 per 100,000 aged over one but less than two years old. In their review of the evidence, NICE (2009) cite the findings from two systematic reviews (Foerster *et al.*, 2009; Kemp *et al.*, 2008), which compared abuse head trauma in children with non-abusive head trauma. Intracranial injuries considered in the studies were: subdural haemorrhage (a form of traumatic brain injury in which blood gathers within the inner meningeal layer of the dura mater – the outer protective covering of the brain); subarachnoid haemorrhage (bleeding into the subarachnoid space – the area between the arachnoid membrane and the pia mater surrounding the brain); and traumatic brain injury as well as associated features such as retinal haemorrhages (the abnormal bleeding of the blood vessels in the retina), skulls fractures, skeletal fractures, seizures and apnoea (temporary absence or cessation of breathing). NICE (2009) conclude that there is strong evidence that abusive head injury occurs primarily in babies and infants, and there is a strong association between intracranial injury and retinal haemorrhages, apnoeic episodes and skeletal fractures. More often than not, SCRs involving under-ones are convened because the child has died – a majority of deaths being the result of physical assault (Brandon and Thoburn, 2008). SCRs show that severe physical assault of an infant, usually involving head injury, appears in up to 50% of all maltreatment-related deaths and serious injuries involving under-ones (Brandon *et al.*, 2009) and is the commonest cause of abuse-related deaths (Brandon *et al.*, 2011) or long-term disability from maltreatment (Sidebotham and Fleming, 2007).

NAHI tends to encompass a more general definition of abusive head trauma and non-accidental head injuries to children, and includes Shaken Baby Syndrome (SBS). Although the American Academy of Paediatrics Committee on Child Abuse and Neglect and Committee on Community Health Services (1999) classifies SBS as 'a clearly definable medical condition', there has been considerable controversy surrounding its definition and diagnosis (Duhaime *et al.*, 1987). Recognising the advances in understanding the pathology and range of disruptive mechanisms to the brain and spinal cord, the Academy has now called for a less mechanistic terminology than SBS, preferring instead 'abusive head trauma' (Christian *et al.*, 2009). While the NICE (2009) guidance makes no specific reference to SBS, it was first identified in the medical literature by Caffy (1946). Since then, SBS has been given a number of other labels, including: shaken impact syndrome; shaking injury; whiplash shaking injury; abusive head trauma and NAHI (David, 2001). Abusive head trauma and NAHI tend to encompass a more general definition of head injuries to children, which include SBS. The characteristic injuries associated with SBS include retinal haemorrhages, multiple fractures of the long bones, and subdural hematomas. While the American Academy of Paediatrics Committee on Child Abuse and Neglect and Committee on Community Health Services (1999) classifies SBS as 'a clearly definable medical condition', there has been considerable controversy surrounding the definition and diagnosis of SBS. Most notably, research by Duhaime *et al.* (1987) suggested that, while shaking may be part of the process, it is the impact of a baby's head against a hard or soft surface which is responsible for the resulting damage to the brain. Prange *et al.*'s (2003) analysis further questioned the existence of non-impact SBS, and subsequent arguments have been made concerning the lack of clinical data on shaking induced brain injury and the relationship between shaking and retinal haemorrhage (Biron and Skelton, 2005). There is also some controversy around whether shaking alone can cause traumatic brain injury, and there is still strong medical support for the diagnosis of SBS (Kemp *et al.*, 2003; Barr *et al.*, 2009). A number of international studies have identified a significant incidence of cases in which perpetrators actually admitted shaking the child (Dias *et al.*, 2005; Barr *et al.*, 2009). Equally, an in-depth qualitative UK study, which explored the prevalence of shaking with a community sample of eighty-three mothers, found that 10% reported having actually shaken their babies, with a further quarter saying that they had felt like doing so (Russell *et al.*, 2008).

PHYSICAL EFFECTS OF VIOLENCE

Health professionals are advised by NICE (2009) to suspect maltreatment if a child presents with physical injuries such as bruises, bites, burns, fractures and head injuries in the absence of major trauma and where there is no suitable explanation as to how the injuries might have occurred. An injury to a child who is not independently mobile is listed as one of the factors that should trigger maltreatment suspicions and is of particular relevance to infants. Other injuries such as fractures, NAHI and shaking injuries are all physical injuries to children which have particular relevance to infants

Fractures

A systematic review (Kemp *et al.*, 2008) highlights that skeletal fractures are diagnosed in up to one-third of children who have been investigated for physical abuse. These fractures often occur in infants and toddlers who cannot give an explanation and are often occult in nature, when the fracture does not show up on a standard X-ray immediately after trauma to a bone; in many cases, it may appear on subsequent X-rays because of loss of bone around the fracture during the healing process. Children who have been physically abused represent a small proportion of the total number of childhood fractures. Nonetheless, health professionals need to be able to recognise the characteristics of fractures resulting from abuse and to initiate the appropriate child-protection procedures. Fractures related to abuse were most commonly recorded in infants and toddlers, with rib fractures and humeral fractures having the highest probability of being inflicted through abuse. Multiple fractures were also more common in cases of abuse. The NICE guidance (2009) concludes that, when infants and toddlers present with a fracture in the absence of a confirmed cause, physical abuse should be considered as a potential cause. However, no fracture, on its own, can distinguish an abusive from a non-abusive cause, and assessment of individual fractures, the site, fracture type and developmental stage of the child is required to help determine the likelihood of abuse.

Physical punishment and physical abuse

There is clear evidence to suggest that the physical punishment of children in the UK remains widespread. In a research review (Ghate, 2000), more than half of the parents (58%) reported using minor physical punishment on their children in the year that the study was conducted; while 9% admitted using severe physical punishment on their children. In the same study, seven in ten parents reported using minor physical punishment with their children at some point in their childhood. In the NSPCC prevalence study (Cawson *et al.*, 2000), 10% of young adults interviewed reported experiencing routine physical punishment, declining only slightly ten years later (Radford *et al.*, 2011). In addition, we also know that instances of physical abuse that come to the attention of the authorities are often justified and explained by parents as physical punishment that has escalated or got out of hand. Despite clear changes in media representations of physical punishment (Redman and Taylor, 2006) and a change in attitude across much of mainland Europe, the UK remains reluctant to acknowledge the potential linkages between physical punishment and physical abuse. While for most parents a small 'smack' is harmless, there is no evidence to show it is effective as a means of discipline (Taylor and Redman, 2004).

Physical violence between peers

To date, most research into physical abuse have tended to concentrate on abuse of children at home by their parents or carers. There have been few studies of children's experiences of violence in settings other than home; for example, at school, in the street or in sport or leisure settings. Prior research has not tended to look at children's overall experiences of violence across these settings. In addition, most studies have focused primarily on children's experiences of physical abuse by adults. Some information on these issues is beginning to emerge (Radford *et al.*, 2011; Turner *et al.*, 2006). Research has also highlighted that, when children and young people themselves are asked about physical harm, their concerns are mainly around violence from peers. Their fears are of street violence, in playgrounds and in unsupervised spaces in sport or leisure settings. Young people report being preoccupied by this on a daily basis, often carrying high levels of fear (Barter *et al.*, 2009).

Female genital mutilation

> 'It is my hope that we can see the abolition of [female genital mutilation/cutting] even sooner than within a generation, but no later than within a generation, and that we also do everything we can to create conditions for every child, girl, and boy, to have the chance to live up to his or her ... potential.' (Clinton, 2012)

Female genital mutilation/cutting (FGM/C) (sometimes referred to as female circumcision) has been practised in various forms for centuries. It is defined as: 'all procedures involving partial or total removal of the external female genitalia or other injury to the female genital organs for non-medical reasons' (World Health Organization, 2008).

There is great variation in FGM/C prevalence between and within countries, reflecting ethnicity and tradition. FGM/C is accepted practice in twenty-eight countries in Africa and in a few countries in Asia and the Middle East. It is estimated that at least two million girls under the age of fifteen are cut each year. In the UK each year it has been estimated that more than 20,000 girls under the age of fifteen are at risk of FGM/C, and that 66,000 women in the UK are living with the consequences of FGM/C. However, the true extent is unknown due to the 'hidden' nature of the crime (HM Government, 2011). Despite the harm it causes, many women from FGM/C-practising communities consider FGM/C normal, and necessary, to protect their 'cultural identity' (FORWARD, 2009). Those who are affected by FGM/C may be British citizens born to parents from FGM/C-practising communities or else women resident in the UK who were born in countries that practice FGM/C. These may include immigrants, refugees, asylum seekers, overseas students and the wives of overseas students. In the majority of cases, FGM/C takes place between the ages of five and eight. These figures were based on the 2001 census and are likely to have increased since then, because of migration to the UK from practising countries.

FGM/C has been classified by the World Health Organization into four types

Type 1 – Clitoridectomy: partial or total removal of the clitoris (a small, sensitive and erectile part of the female genitals) and, in very rare cases, only the prepuce (the fold of skin surrounding the clitoris).

Type 2 – Excision: partial or total removal of the clitoris and the labia minora, with or without excision of the labia majora (the labia are the 'lips' that surround the vagina).

Type 3 – Infibulation: narrowing of the vaginal opening through the creation of a covering seal. The seal is formed by cutting and repositioning the inner, or outer, labia, with or without removal of the clitoris.

Type 4 – Other: all other harmful procedures to the female genitalia for non-medical purposes, e.g. pricking, piercing, incising, scraping and cauterising the genital area.

FGM/C is illegal and, however well intentioned, it is both an act of child cruelty and a violation of the child's human rights. It serves no medical purpose whatsoever. Although FGM/C was first prohibited in Britain in 1988, practising communities continued to take children abroad for the procedure until legislation in 2003 made this an offence. Depending on the degree of mutilation, the consequences of FGM/C can be fatal (FORWARD, 2009). However, safeguarding girls at risk of harm through FGM/C poses specific challenges because the families involved may give no other cause for concern: for example, with regard to their parenting responsibilities or relationships with their children (HM Government, 2011).

Short-term consequences of FGM/C can include:

- severe pain and shock;
- urine retention;
- infection;
- injury to adjacent tissues:
- immediate fatal haemorrhaging.

In addition to these health consequences, there are considerable psychosexual, psychological and social consequences of FGM. Thus, long-term implications can include:

- extensive damage of the external reproductive system;
- uterine, vaginal and pelvic infections;
- increased risk of HIV infection;
- cysts and neuromas;
- increased risk of Vesicovaginal fistula;
- complications in pregnancy and childbirth;
- psychological damage;
- psychological damage, including a number of mental-health and psychosexual problems such as low libido, depression, anxiety and sexual dysfunction; flashbacks during pregnancy and childbirth; substance misuse and/or self-harm;
- renal impairment and possible renal failure.

Recent approaches suggest it is more appropriate to refer to female genital cutting (FGC), because mutilation is a value-laden term that is likely to upset young women further, and be deemed a judgement on what some might call a cultural practice. Referring to the practice as female circumcision is also a misnomer. Although beyond the scope of this book, FGC is a serious issue of physical abuse. The Orchid Project (http://orchidproject.org/category/about-fgc/what-is-fgc; accessed 24 June 2014) and others provide useful information.

Feldman-Jacobs and Clifton (2014) illustrate how the last decade of research and interventions has yielded invaluable lessons on what programmes and policies are effective in moving towards abandonment of FGM/C. They fall into three broad categories:

- The centrality of social norms – what communities believe and how they act and expect the members of that community to act – has gained wide recognition as key to FGM/C abandonment.

- A wide range of actors play pivotal roles in the abandonment of FGM/C – men, women, grandmothers, boys and girls, as well as community, religious and political leaders.
- The focus must be on holistic, integrated, multi-sectoral approaches that bring together the advocacy, policy-level work, and on community-level transformation of social norms.

FABRICATED AND INDUCED ILLNESS

Although child maltreatment due to abuse or neglect is pervasive within our society, less is known about fabricated or induced illness (FII) by carers, a rare form of child abuse (Lazenbatt and Taylor, 2011). FII occurs when a caregiver (usually the mother) falsifies illness in a child by fabricating or producing symptoms and presenting the child for medical care, disclaiming knowledge of the cause of the problem, with the purpose of obtaining an emotional or psychological benefit (Rosenburg, 1987; Schreier and Libow, 1993). FII usually occurs in infants and children under the age of five years, with newborns the most likely to be harmed (Feldman *et al.*, 2001; Lazenbatt and Taylor, 2011; 2013). They can experience unnecessary investigations and treatment when subject to FII; induced illness can itself cause death. Feldman (2004) argues that it is a much wider phenomenon than just 'a form of child abuse taking place in a medical setting', as manifestations of FII can be seen in the community at large. Likewise, physical symptoms are only a part of the spectrum of FII, with other kinds of 'problems' (e.g. psychological and mental-health symptoms) that are exaggerated, fabricated or induced in some cases. Findings suggest that up to 10% of these children die, and about 50% experience long-term impairment of their physical, psychological and emotional development (Lasher and Sheridan, 2004; Lazenbatt and Taylor, 2013).

However, FII may be seen as an exception in 'high risk' families, as it is perpetrated by all social classes and is not always associated with other types of family violence or crime, nor is it connected with young, inexperienced parents or socio-economic deprivation (NICE, 2009). Also, although the primary responsibility rests with the abusive carer, health professionals can play an important part in its evolution and in the iatrogenic harm caused to the child (Lazenbatt and Taylor, 2011; Bass and Jones, 2011).

Carer behaviour can include:

- deliberately inducing symptoms in children by administering medication or other substances, or by means of intentional suffocation;
- interfering with treatments by overdosing, not administering them or interfering with medical equipment such as infusion lines;
- claiming that the child has symptoms which are difficult to prove unless observed directly, such as pain, frequency of passing urine, vomiting or fits. These claims result in unnecessary investigations and treatments, which may cause secondary physical problems;
- exaggerating symptoms, causing professionals to undertake investigations and treatments which may be invasive, are unnecessary and therefore are harmful and possibly dangerous;
- obtaining specialist treatments or equipment for children who do not require them;
- claiming a psychological illness in a child.

The benefits for the carer are usually in the form of support provided by family, friends and society, particularly when others view them as grief-stricken, brave or heroic for the manner in which they attend to the child-victim's medical care and deal with the perceived seriousness of the child's illness.

Feldman *et al.* (2001) argue that it is a much wider phenomenon than just 'a form of child abuse taking place in a medical setting'. Manifestations of FII can be seen in schools, churches, the legal system, child protection agencies, the home and the community at large. Likewise, physical symptoms are only a part of the spectrum of FII, with other kinds of 'problems' (e.g. psychological and mental-health symptoms) that are exaggerated, fabricated or induced in some cases. FII is perpetrated by all social classes and is not always associated with other types of family violence or crime, nor is it connected with young, inexperienced parents or socio-economic deprivation. Although FII is uncommon, it has a high morbidity and is often not recognised until the child has suffered a great deal, both physically and emotionally. The increased risk of unexplained death in siblings of children identified as having fabricated illness (Sheridan, 2002) shows that the syndrome may be under-detected and current methods for identifying it are underdeveloped (Rogers, 2004). A stronger multidisciplinary approach and awareness across universal, medical and legal services is urgently required (Bass and Glaser, 2014).

FILICIDE

In the UK, approximately one or two children die each week at the hands of their parents (Brandon *et al.*, 2011). Over the past decade numerous studies have examined rates and characteristics of filicide, in an attempt to understand why, in order to find ways to prevent future filicide events (West *et al.*, 2009; Porter and Gavin, 2010). Researchers have attempted to establish possible motivations (Resnick, 1970), highlight perpetrator characteristics (Lindberg *et al.*, 2009) and examine the influence of mental illness (Rosenbaum, 1990; Flynn *et al.*, 2013).

Filicide followed by the suicide of the perpetrator is not routinely recorded as a discrete category of child abuse or child death, so its incidence is particularly difficult to establish. While filicide-suicide seems relatively rare, the sudden and violent nature of the incident can impact seriously on the lives of large numbers of people, including family, wider extended family, friends and the community. Despite anecdotal information suggesting that it may be on the increase, and despite it being one of the most drastic forms of child abuse, often followed by intense media interest and reporting, filicide-suicide remains a rarely studied phenomenon. We know little about the aetiology and antecedents for this kind of behaviour.

Filicide-suicide is often triggered by an event considered by the perpetrator to be a great loss – often sexual jealousy, sometimes financial. Sometimes, the incident occurs at the point at which a woman leaves a violent relationship when the man appears to take 'revenge' by harming the children in a gesture of 'if I cannot have them no one will'. It can also be associated with mental illness, drug addiction and poor financial prospects. Filicide-suicide can be an act of 'no hope', where someone feels they have nothing left to lose. It is sometimes justified as being a benefit to the children; taking them out of something into something better. This is sometimes referred to as 'misplaced altruism'. Although there is increasing research about the motivations for filicide-suicide, caution needs to be exerted as we cannot know what occurs in the minds of people who then kill themselves.

Conclusion

In this chapter we have taken a closer look at violence and its effects on children and infants and the overwhelming evidence between living with violence and being killed. We looked at NAHI and some of the controversies around SBS. We explored the range of injuries a physically abused child might experience and then considered the linkages between physical punishment and physical abuse. Violence between peers is an increasing area of interest and research, as is that of FGC and FII. Finally, some of the research examining filicide-suicide was explored.

CHAPTER 3

Theorising maltreatment

Introduction

In this chapter we examine some of the major theories that help us understand maltreatment in high risk families. We base our understanding of child maltreatment within an ecological framework. The explosion of research on neurodevelopment is then explored, alongside the effects of post-traumatic stress and the importance of strong attachment relationships. There are strong associations between childhood abuse and mental ill health, both as a child and an adult. Impoverished environments can further exacerbate vulnerability for children, and inter-generational cycles of violence are not uncommon.

> ... maltreated children are likely to manifest atypicalities in neurobiological processes, physiological responsiveness, emotion recognition and emotion regulation, attachment relationships, self-system development, representational processes, social information processing, peer relationships, school functioning, and romantic relationships (Cicchetti, 2013, p. 403).

Major advances in neuroscience, molecular biology, genomics and the behavioural and social sciences are deepening our understanding of healthy development in the child. Infancy and the child's experiences during these early years lay a foundation of learning, behaviour, building relationships and overall mental health and well-being. A strong foundation in these early years lays the matrix for economic prosperity, healthy communities and successful parenting of the next generation. However, a weak foundation can seriously undermine the social and economic vitality of a nation (Thornberry *et al.*, 2012). Over many decades research in child development has taught us that parents, families and communities provide the much needed supportive relationships and positive learning experiences that young children need for healthy development (Shonkoff and Phillips, 2000). Unhealthy child development occurs with toxic stress in early childhood including violence, domestic abuse, substance misuse and parental mental health, which can establish a vicious cycle of stress, impairing the child's development of critical cognitive, social and emotional skills, and prompting behavioural and physiological adaptations in an ongoing attempt to cope.

SOCIO-ECOLOGICAL FRAMEWORKS

There is no single factor alone that can account for why some people behave violently to children or why child abuse is more prevalent in some communities than in others (Butchart *et al.*, 2006). Researchers over the last three decades have studied the contribution of theories of the inter-relationships between the individual and environment and how they impact on child outcomes, with specific emphasis on child maltreatment (Bronfenbrenner, 1979). Bronfenbrenner's socio-ecological theory hypothesises that multiple layers of risk from individual to wider societal risks must be taken into consideration when attempting to understand the antecedents and consequences of child abuse (Belsky *et al.*, 2010). These developmental theories allow the investigation of correlational and causal relationships among risk factors associated with child abuse (Cicchetti, 2014). Maltreatment is therefore probably best understood by analysing the complex interactions between the numbers of factors at different levels.

Socio-ecological models have been accepted as useful in examining risk factors for child abuse for a number of years (Black *et al.*, 2001). This approach stems from Bronfenbrenner's ecological model (Bronfenbrenner, 1979) of human development. This distinguishes between proximal factors, which are the primary and immediate processes for influencing development in the day-to-day life of a child, such as parent–child relationships, and distal factors in the immediate and wider context, such as the school, community and wider society. The framework suggests a nested model of spheres of influence to represent the developing child's interaction with their family, community and wider environment, which can both contribute to and compensate for risk factors operating at other levels. The interpretation by the World Health Organization (Butchart *et al.*, 2006) is probably the most comprehensive framework (see Figure 1).

Socio-ecology has now emerged as one of the dominant meta-paradigms for understanding childhood experience and early relationships (Bronfenbrenner, 1979; 1986), including the short- and

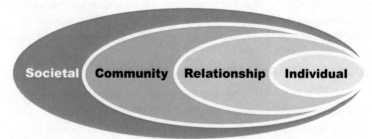

Figure 1: Socio-ecological nested model (adapted from Butchart *et al.*, 2006).

long-term effects of childhood abuse and neglect (e.g. Cicchetti and Toth, 2005; Cicchetti and Valentino, 2006; Belsky *et al.*, 2010; Cicchetti, 2014). The socio-ecological framework model emphasises the fact that child maltreatment occurs within the context of relationships between a perpetrator(s) and a victim(s), and this maltreatment is seen as being situated with 'pathogenic relational environments' (Cicchetti and Toth, 2005).

There is a range of levels that might contribute to the maltreatment and neglect of children. They include the following.

Individual level
This level includes the child and his/her parents/caregivers and deals with biological variables (e.g. age, gender) and with personal history factors that can influence susceptibility to maltreatment. Infant risk factors at this level include premature birth, constant and persistent crying, attachment difficulties and disability.

Relationship level
Close personal relationships can influence the risk of both perpetrating and being a victim of maltreatment. Stressors, which families sometimes face, include family disruptions, domestic violence, mental health, substance abuse and financial difficulties. Cyr *et al.* (2010) undertook a meta-analysis of risks of maltreatment in families and noted that socio-economic risks are pervasive, tending to characterise a family for a prolonged amount of time (e.g. poverty, adolescent parenting), and also having a propensity to co-occur and cluster in the same families and individuals.

Community level

This includes factors such as neighbourhoods and schools and the characteristics within those that might contribute to maltreatment: for example, prevailing norms about the treatment and status of children, and economic and social circumstances and access to employment.

Macro-cultural level

These comprise social and economic policy settings, including poverty, and social norms encouraging harsh punishments, economic inequalities and absence of social welfare nets. Comprehensive models for child protection include interventions at all levels of the ecological model.

The AAP has recently released a technical report that proposes an eco-bio-developmental (EBD) framework for understanding the ongoing evolution of an individual's strengths and risks for health over his or her lifespan (Shonkoff, 2011). Importantly, new evidence suggests that prolonged exposure to the stress response with release of cortisol and adrenaline can be toxic to the developing infant brain, rendering it more susceptible to excessive or prolonged stress throughout the life course (Shonkoff, 2010). The EBD framework argues in a similar way to the economist James Heckman (Heckman *et al.*, 2006), believing that investments in families with children are the right thing to do, both morally and scientifically, as the biological mechanisms underlying the well-established associations between early childhood adversity and lifelong disparities in learning, behaviour and health are becoming increasingly clear (Heckman, 2008; Shonkoff *et al.*, 2012; Garner *et al.*, 2012).

Shonkoff *et al.* (2012) have built on this model by designing a more policy-driven EBD framework, which informs the development of early childhood interventions and services. This model expands on Bronfenbrenner's ecological model and combines it with a bio-developmental framework (Bronfenbrenner, 1979) developed by Shonkoff (2010) to offer an integrated, evidence-based approach to coordinated, early childhood policymaking and practice across sectors. From a public health perspective, this model also takes account of national policies and programmes, voluntary and community resources, and the physical and relational context in which families live, together with the individual genetic/biological and environmental influences which can impact on health and well-being.

NEUROBIOLOGY AND NEURODEVELOPMENT

> Early developmental experiences with caregivers, the infant's first exposure to humans, create a set of associations and 'templates' for the child's brain about what humans are. Are humans safe, predictable? Are they a source of sustenance, comfort, and pleasure? Or are they unpredictable and a source of fear, chaos, pain, and loss? (Perry and Hambrick, 2008).

Over the last fifteen years, advances in neurobiology and neurodevelopment have illuminated some of our understanding of the impact of child maltreatment (Perry *et al.*, 1995; Perry, 1996; Shonkoff, 2010; Shonkoff *et al.*, 2012). The science of epigenetics provides a biological link between early childhood ecology and the way the developmental blueprint is read. Epigenetics literally means 'above the genome' and refers to the molecular mechanisms, such as DNA, that determine which genes get turned on, when and where. Epigenetics is critical because inheriting a gene that makes one more susceptible to being addicted to substances (or being violent or depressed) is not much of a risk if that gene is never turned on.

Advances in epigenetics demonstrate that the ecology literally alters the way the genetic programme is utilised, not only in the current generation, but also in the next as well (Shonkoff and Phillips, 2000; Perry, 2002; 2011; Shonkoff *et al.*, 2012). Findings from this work show through sophisticated brain imaging how the foetal and infant brain is developing and shaped through a constant interaction with the external ecology or environment. This childhood ecology literally sculpts the foundational architecture of the developing brain. This development is rapid in the perinatal period and in the first year of life and continues for the child's first four years. At birth, the human brain is undeveloped. The brain matures during childhood, with brain-related capabilities developing in a sequential fashion: infants crawl before they can walk; babble before they can talk (Perry, 1996).

The most regulatory, lower regions of the brain develop first; followed, in sequence, by adjacent but higher, more complex regions. This process of sequential development is guided by experience: the brain develops and modifies itself in response to experience with neurons and neuronal connections (synapses) changing in an activity-dependent fashion (Perry *et al.*, 1995; Perry, 1998). Jordan and Sketchley (2009) have characterised this symbiotic relationship between brain development and environmental stimuli as the process by which 'states' become 'traits'. Thus, although inherited genetic potential predisposes children to certain characteristics, skills and abilities, it is environmental influences and contexts that determine the ultimate expression of these potentials (Jordan and Sketchley, 2009).

We know there is a symbiotic relationship between brain development and environmental stimuli, and new technologies such as functional magnetic resonance imaging (MRI) and positron emission tomography (PET) have enabled researchers to identify the chemical and structural differences between the central nervous systems of abused and non-abused young children (Teicher, 2000; Neigh *et al.*, 2009). They can also show that connections among neurons in these inactivated regions can literally wither away, hampering the child's functioning later in life (Teicher *et al.*, 2004; Weniger *et al.*, 2008). This new evidence tells us that early exposure to maltreatment, stress and trauma causes physical effects on an infant's neurodevelopment, which may lead to changes in their long-term response to stress and vulnerability to later mental-health disorders (De Bellis, 2001; 2005; Glaser, 2007; Schore, 2009).

Maltreatment has therefore been identified as a risk factor for inhibiting the appropriate development of certain regions of the brain (Glaser, 2000; Jordan and Sketchley, 2009). Two wide-ranging reviews of research conclude that 'there is considerable evidence for changes in brain function in association with child abuse and neglect' (Glaser, 2000, p. 110); and: 'It is clear that early deleterious experiences can have significant negative effects on the developing brain that may be long-term' (Nelson and Bosquet, 2000, p. 46). Indeed, neglected infants may not be exposed to stimuli that normally activate important regions of the brain and strengthen cognitive pathways. The connections among neurons in these inactivated regions can literally wither away, hampering the child's functioning later in life (Rutter, 1979a). As a result, the brain may become 'wired' to experience the world as hostile and uncaring.

This negative perspective may influence the infant's later interactions, prompting them to become anxious and overly aggressive or emotionally withdrawn (Fonagy *et al.*, 2002a). Evidence also suggests that the link between maltreatment and adverse health consequences can develop through a stress or anxiety response, which can influence the nervous and immune systems, causing alteration of the function of the hypothalamic–pituitary–adrenal axis (HPA) axis (Widom and Maxfield, 2001; Glaser, 2002; Neigh *et al.*, 2009), and for some children a level of hyper-arousal that can continue throughout their lives. The HPA axis is not fully developed at birth and is thus subject to environmental experiences that shape its activity.

Most infants experience a decline in HPA activity during preschool years as they learn to cope with stressors, identify most threats as mild, and receive appropriate and supportive feedback from parents. However, infants and young children faced with abusive parents may be at risk for poor regulation of the HPA axis (Weniger *et al.*, 2008), as these infants often do not have access to parental support to regulate and manage their stress. This places them at risk of experiencing severe and more chronic states of stress that can have long-term negative consequences on functioning (Schore, 2001). Importantly, these processes offer some explanation of how and why stress may continue to impact on outcomes long after the abuse itself may have ended.

Many longer-term health problems, including anxiety, panic or PTSD, chronic fatigue syndrome, fibromyalgia, depression, some auto-immune disorders, suicidal tendencies and abnormal fear responses, can be understood, in some cases, as manifestations of child trauma and maltreatment (Kendall-Tackett, 2001; De Bellis, 2005). Nonetheless, a secure attachment to a primary caregiver in early life seems still to be the most protective factor that can be offered to children.

Infants are particularly vulnerable to the effects of abuse and neglect in the first years of life. Detrimental early experiences and subsequent neurobiological damage can cause an infant to develop a range of problems, such as learning disability, language delay, lack of empathy, hyperactivity associated with disruptive behaviour and distractibility or hyper-vigilance (Gilbert *et al.*, 2009) as well as emotional difficulties stemming from poor impulse control (Schore, 2001). Infants and toddlers are at greatest risk of serious injury, and are often the most difficult cases to recognise because of absence of available history from the victim (Woodman *et al.*, 2011). Physical abuse is associated with various types of injuries and lack of parental attachments, particularly when exposure to such abuse occurs in the first three years of life (Sousa *et al.*, 2011). It is estimated that 10% of admissions to paediatric burns and plastic surgery units are related to child maltreatment and abuse (Chester *et al.*, 2006).

It should be noted that there is an emergent critique of the neuroscience and early years debate. The emphasis on the early years in policy and practice in the UK is unprecedented and it is certainly a positive trend. However, the idea that a baby's brain is irrevocably shaped during the early years does not take account of the other critical development phase during adolescence. It also suggests a biological determinism that sees a very small window for opportunity and recovery.

> The connections made are endless: babies who fail to make the right neural connections will do badly at school, lack empathy, succumb to criminality, have mental-health problems, and end up in a cycle of deprivation themselves (Williams, 2014).

Recent years have seen mental-health professionals from clinical perspectives consider psychiatric treatment approaches for childhood PTSD (possible result of child abuse), weaving this in with developmental neuroscience research on the biological aspects of attachment theory. One objective is to attempt to reverse some of the brain impairments that may have resulted from chronic stress by providing positive experiences. Thus, in addition to psychological and family treatment goals, there are psychobiological goals such as decreasing stress reactivity and modifying brain connections through new experiences (Twardosz and Lutzker, 2010). Brain plasticity is seen as an important concept in this field: the ability of the brain to respond to experience by modifying its structure and function, both during development and throughout life. This is a reassuring counter to some of the determinism imbued by the first 1,001 days agenda – it is possible to recover from childhood abuse.

Glaser's reviews (2000, 2007) emphasise that different types of abuse and other types of trauma may affect the development of brain systems that regulate responsiveness to stress in ways that may be maladaptive to mental health. In addition, some types of maltreatment, most especially neglect, result in a lack of experiences needed for typical brain development. Early exposure to stress and trauma, including fear of violence, causes physical effects on neurodevelopment which may lead to changes in the individual's long-term response to stress and vulnerability to psychiatric disorders (Lubit *et al.,* 2003).

There are significant concerns about the development of PTSD in children who have been abused in childhood. Nearly a third of victims of childhood maltreatment meet DSM-III-R criteria for lifetime PTSD (Widom, 1999). The *Diagnostic and Statistical Manual of Mental Disorders* (American Psychiatric Association, 2011) provides a common language and standard criteria for the classification of mental disorders. However, while victims of child maltreatment are at increased risk for developing PTSD, childhood maltreatment is not a sufficient condition. Family, individual and lifestyle variables also place individuals at risk and contribute to the symptoms of PTSD. Thus, the general effects of other family variables (such as poverty, parental alcoholism or drug problems, or other inadequate social and family functioning) need to be disentangled from specific sequelae associated with childhood abuse (Widom, 1999).

Previous research has suggested that abused and neglected children are at increased risk of early behaviour problems and conduct disorder (Breslau and Davis, 1987; Widom, 1999), while behaviour problems in childhood or adolescence may be associated with increased risk for engaging in risky behaviours. In turn, such behaviours may lead to increased risk of exposure to traumatic events and to subsequent PTSD. Another possibility is that childhood maltreatment may be associated with PTSD through its effect on a person's lifestyle, which places the person more or less at risk for exposure to traumatic events and, ultimately, PTSD. It is difficult though to disentangle what this might mean for child abuse specifically, as opposed to maltreatment in general.

ATTACHMENT THEORY AND DEVELOPMENT

> The single most effective way to stop producing people with
> the propensity to violence is to ensure infants are reared in
> an environment that fosters their development of empathy.
> The surest way to achieve this is by supporting parents in
> developing attachment and attunement with their infants
> (Hosking and Walsh, 2005).

The earliest years of life are a critical period when infants and young children are making socio-emotional attachments and forming the crucial first relationships, which lay the foundations for future mental health and well-being (Schore, 2011). One of the most important and universal tasks during the early years is for the child to develop a strong attachment to their primary caregiver. Attachment is defined as the biologically predisposed, enduring, emotional connection that keeps the child in proximity to the caregiver through the vulnerable early years (Bowlby, 1969; Ainsworth, 1979) and provides security to allow their social, emotional, physical, cognitive, language, temperament and fine and gross motor skills to develop. Attachment theory (Bowlby, 1978; 1979; 1988; Ainsworth, 1979; Schore, 2009; 2011) suggests that our early relationship experiences, especially the responses of our main caregiver/s, may have a far-reaching influence on our subsequent relationships and how we view ourselves, the world and other people. Attachment theory has developed over many years and has transformed itself from a bio-psychosocial (Harlow, 1971) and behavioural theory (Ainsworth et al., 1978) to a cognitive theory and now, to a psycho-neurobiological theory of development (Schore, 2009). These theory developments are revolutionising our views of early child development, psychopathology, neurobiology and trauma and clinical work with young children and their families (Fonagy et al., 2002b; Schore, 2010).

Feeling secure, loved and having a safe base from which to explore, and return to, are ongoing needs met by the parent–caregiver relationship. Numerous studies, including some of the most comprehensive and well controlled (Cicchetti, 2013; 2014) have demonstrated that a secure attachment style is most associated with parental behaviours that are consistently responsive to the child's needs and provide comfort during times of distress (Bowlby and King, 2004). This results in numerous positive outcomes over the course of development, including positive emotional and behavioural functioning, academic success, effective peer relationships and few behaviour problems (Cicchetti and Toth, 2005; Cicchetti, 2013). Though almost all infants develop an attachment relationship to their primary caregiver(s), not all of them are able to use their caregiver(s) as a secure base or haven of safety from which to explore the world. Important early developmental tasks involve the regulation of emotion that allows a child to cope with stress, control impulse and rage, and to develop empathy (Fonagy *et al.*, 2002b). Emotional development is most often achieved in the context of a secure attachment. However, children who have not been able to develop these healthy attachments have not laid the necessary groundwork for positive emotional development and may have a limited capacity for empathy (Butchart *et al.*, 2006).

The critical period for attachment formation coincides with the period of the most rapid brain maturation. Therefore, exposure to trauma such as maltreatment and abuse affects every dimension of a young child's cognitive, psychosocial and emotional development as well as their attachment relationships through the life course (Schore, 2011). Reviews have highlighted the long-term negative effects that maltreatment can have on both bonding and attachment behaviours (see Cicchetti and Toth, 2005; Cicchetti and Valentino, 2006; Cicchetti, 2013). If a parent or caregiver is not seen as reliable and responsive, then the infant's ability to develop feelings of security in his or her primary attachment relationship is likely to be seriously impeded (Bowlby and King, 2004).

Exposure to multiple high risk and trauma (e.g. abuse, domestic abuse, violence, fear) affects every dimension of an infant's psychological functioning and attachment (Perry, 2002; Lubit *et al.*, 2003). As a result, very young abused or neglected infants may be overwhelmed with intense negative emotions, manifesting in incessant crying, inability to be soothed, feeding problems, sleep disturbances, hyper-arousal and hyper-vigilance, as well as intense distress during transitions. Toddlers and younger children may experience intense separation anxiety, wariness of strangers, social avoidance and withdrawal, and constricted and repetitive play (Jordan and Sketchley, 2009; Neigh *et al.*, 2009). They are likely to have reduced tolerance of frustration as well as problems with emotional regulation, as evident in intractable tantrums, non-compliance and negativism, aggression and controlling behaviour. Extreme anxiety may be expressed as new fears, constricted and repetitive play, hyper-vigilance, reckless and accident-prone behaviour, and fear of body damage. While attachment theory is persuasive for the very early years, it is acknowledged that there remain questions about its efficacy in older children and with caregivers other than the mother.

Research has shown that children who live in high risk families may not have secure attachment relationships early in life and are therefore at risk of significant mental-health problems, educational difficulties and conduct disorders (Cicchetti, 2013). Hesse and Main (2006) have suggested that these behaviours characterise infants with a disorganised attachment style and may be the result of fear in approaching a possibly maltreating or traumatised caregiver who must also be called on to provide comfort. Moreover, longitudinal and retrospective studies cited by Balbernie (2008) link disorganised emotional attachment in infancy, as a consequence of abuse and neglect, to a number of severe psycho-pathological responses and mental-health problems in adulthood, such as depression, severe anxiety, addictions, drug and alcohol abuse, PTSD, self-harm and suicide as well as being bullied.

Emotional neglect and early childhood deprivation are potentially the most severe risk factors for impaired emotional or intellectual development and are also found as cofactors in most cases of other types of child maltreatment. Neglected infants with disorganised attachments have been found to have more severe cognitive and academic deficits, social withdrawal and limited peer interactions when compared with those who have been physically abused (Radford *et al.*, 2011). The infant suffers either from quantitatively inadequate emotional support, or else from only weak support, delivered by constantly changing individuals. Emotional neglect leads to educational underachievement and difficulties in peer relationships as well as to oppositional behaviour (Jordan and Sketchley, 2009).

CHILDREN'S MENTAL HEALTH AND WELL-BEING

The earliest years of life are a critical period when infants and young children are making socio-emotional attachments and forming the crucial first relationships, which lay the foundations for future mental health (Bowlby, 1969; Bowlby, 1988). Adverse emotional development in these early years may be associated with various psychosocial risk factors of relevance to the mother and her partner (Sousa et al., 2011). The major factors have been: low educational level of the parents; living with poverty; parental mental-health disorders; alcohol and drug misuse; domestic violence; stress; early parenthood; experience of maltreatment and sexual abuse; unwanted pregnancy; and lack of social support.

Good mental health, emotional, social and psychological well-being help protect young people against emotional and behavioural problems, violence and crime, teenage pregnancy and the misuse of drugs and alcohol (NICE, 2009; Thornberry et al., 2013). It can also help them to learn and achieve academically, thus affecting their long-term social and economic well-being. Young people's mental health and well-being are influenced by a range of factors, from their individual make-up and family background to the community within which they live and society at large, including child maltreatment. While mental-health problems/disorders may account for a large proportion of the disease burden in children and young people in all societies (Office for National Statistics, 2014), they constitute a relatively neglected aspect of public health (Department of Health, 2014. This is despite their importance in the primary prevention of a range of emotional and psychological problems, and their contribution to poor outcomes in adulthood (Rutter, 2007).

All types of maltreatment can affect a child's emotional, psychological and mental well-being, and these consequences may appear immediately or years later. The immediate and longer-term impact of abuse can include mental-health problems such as anxiety, depression, substance misuse, eating disorders and self-destructive behaviours. Numerous past studies have documented associations between a child's exposure to abuse and neglect with several negative mental-health outcomes including: low self-esteem and depression (Briere, 1996; Heim and Nemeroff, 2001); severe anxiety (Kendler and Gardner, 1998); addictions, drug and alcohol abuse (Sousa et al., 2011); PTSD (Murray, 2006); self-harming behaviours and suicidality (Oates, 2003); and being bullied (Radford et al., 2011). Other psychological and emotional conditions include panic disorder, dissociative disorders, attention-deficit/hyperactivity disorder and reactive attachment disorder (Teicher, 2000; De Bellis and Thomas, 2003; Springer et al., 2007). Longitudinal and retrospective studies cited by Balbernie (2003) link disorganised emotional attachment in infancy, as a consequence of abuse and neglect, to a number of severe mental-health problems in adulthood, such as borderline personality disorder, clinical depression and a large number of controlling or incompetent social behaviours.

However, the evidence shows that those children living with multiple adversities such as poor parenting, living with domestic abuse, parental mental health and substance abuse fare worst (Sabates and Dex, 2012). They highlight the central issue that:

> Children living in families with multiple risks are more likely to have long-term disadvantageous cognitive, behavioural and mental-health consequences (Sabates and Dex, 2012, p. 22).

Poor mental and emotional health is evident, as a long-term study suggests that as many as 80% of young adults who had been abused met the diagnostic criteria for at least one psychiatric disorder by the time they reached age twenty-one (Sousa et al., 2011). These young adults exhibited many problems, including depression, anxiety, eating disorders and suicide attempts (Thornberry et al., 2013). Children who experience rejection or neglect are more likely to develop antisocial traits as they grow up and are more associated with borderline personality disorders and violent behaviour (Schore, 2003). Studies have found abused and neglected adolescents to be at least 25% more likely to experience problems such as delinquency, teen pregnancy, low academic achievement, drug use and mental-health problems (Kelley *et al.,* 1997). Other studies suggest that abused young people are likely to engage in sexual risk-taking as they reach adolescence, thereby increasing their chances of contracting a sexually transmitted disease (Johnson *et al.,* 2006).

Evidence shows that around 50% of people receiving mental-health services report abuse as children. One review found that 'on careful questioning, 50–60% of psychiatric inpatients and 40–60% of outpatients report childhood histories of physical or sexual abuse or both' (Read, 1998). Others have concluded that 'child abuse may have a causative role in the most severe psychiatric conditions' (Sousa *et al.,* 2011). In a review of the literature on childhood trauma and psychosis, Read *et al.* (2005, p. 330) report that symptoms usually associated with psychosis, especially hallucinations, 'are at least as strongly related to childhood abuse and neglect as many other mental-health problems'.

While there are indications that the negative effects on health and development can often (but not always) be reversed, this reversal requires timely identification of the maltreatment and appropriate intervention. The harmful effects vary depending on a number of factors, including the circumstances, personal characteristics of the child and the child's environment (Haegerich and Dahlberg, 2011), and may endure long after the abuse or neglect occurs. Researchers have identified links between child maltreatment with difficulties during infancy such as depression and withdrawal symptoms which are common among children as young as 3 who experienced emotional, physical, or neglect (Edwards *et al.,* 2003). Research suggests that early childhood abuse and trauma can cause a persistent biological state likely to function as a risk factor for the occurrence of mental disorders in later life (Shonkoff, 2011). Due to this fact, the ascertainment of abuse in childhood should be recognised as an important risk factor for the occurrence of mental disorders (Sidebotham and Heron, 2006). Persistent neglect can lead to serious impairment of health and development, and children may experience low self-esteem, feelings of being unloved and isolation.

POVERTY AND CHILD ABUSE

Although significant attempts have been taken to end child poverty in the UK, the proportion of children living in poverty there is higher when compared to a generation ago and higher than the level experienced by most European countries (Hooper *et al.*, 2007). Children living in poverty are at a higher risk of a wide range of adverse experiences and unfavourable outcomes, including maltreatment and most notably physical abuse and neglect by parents (Coulton *et al.*, 1995; Garbarino and Kolstelny, 1992; Waldfogel, 2007). This is of course not to say that all parents living in poverty maltreat their children or that all families experiencing cases of maltreatment live in economic deprivation. They are more likely than affluent parents, however, to encounter a range of issues other than material deprivation that may affect their parenting and 'the role of parents in the relationship between poverty and outcomes for children is less well understood' (Katz, 2007).

The main influence of poverty on parenting appears to be the stress it causes, which in turn disrupts parenting practices and styles (Katz, 2007), though this relationship is far from straightforward. Parenting stress is often conceptualised as the frequency of daily hassles encountered in life (Crnic and Greenberg, 1990; Curenton *et al.*, 2009), and mothers who report high levels of parenting stress seem more likely to abuse and/or neglect their children (Johnson, 2002). Stressed parents are more likely to use harsh parenting practices and therefore increasing negative outcomes for children (Webster-Stratton, 1990).

Neighbourhoods represent an important unit of analysis (Freisthler *et al.*, 2006). Firstly, they may affect the social conditions of individuals living within the community, and, secondly, interventions focused at neighbourhood-level provide a unique potential to inform preventative activities whereas most efforts to reduce child maltreatment focus on changing parental behaviour or more immediate circumstances that may lead to an increased risk of abuse. Communities experiencing greater poverty and a lower ratio of two-parent families had significantly higher rates of child physical abuse in a US study (Drake and Pandey, 1996), while similarly in the UK (Ghate and Hazel, 2002) multiple stresses tended to be experienced by parents living in 'poor environments' or disadvantaged communities and have high levels of physical and mental-health problems. The balance of support was also found very useful. However, UK longitudinal data to track the effects of early childhood intervention into adulthood is limited (McDowell and Lyons, 2009), and poverty is a prevalent and neglected risk factor in primary intervention efforts (Klevens and Whitaker, 2007). Preventative activities at this level are potentially more cost-effective than alternative approaches.

INTER-GENERATIONAL CYCLES

Literature on the inter-generational transmission of child physical abuse suggests that individuals physically abused in childhood are at increased risk of physically abusing their own children (Milner *et al.,* 1990; Coohey and Braun, 1997). Numerous studies have demonstrated the negative effects that physical abuse can have throughout the lifetime, and that these have the potential to change both parenting behaviours and the parenting environment (Duncan *et al.,* 1996). Individuals (and especially women) with a history of childhood physical abuse had significantly higher rates of anxiety disorders, major depression, alcoholic dependence, illicit drug use and antisocial behaviour and were more likely to have one or more such disorders than those without such a history (MacMillan *et al.,* 2001). While there is some indication from these studies that boys and girls respond differently to child physical abuse, few accounts make a meaningful differentiation.

Inter-generational cycles are clear in maltreatment: each life stage has moments when effective interventions can take place, but also when things can be made worse. Risk-taking behaviours as a result of early abuse, e.g. drug taking, can then impact on parenting behaviours and the social environment, which can lead to further abuse. Early interventions are thus crucial, given the developing brain. However, it is important to note that inter-generational cycles of abuse are not inevitable, and there are many stages where decreasing risk factors and increasing protective factors can break this kind of cycle. Much can be learnt from studies where individuals have encountered severe adversity and maltreatment in childhood, yet have not repeated this in their own parenting behaviours (Harris and Dersch, 2001). The majority of physically abused individuals are not violent towards their own children (Kaufman and Zigler, 1987; Widom, 1989). Prospective studies have shown that, while there is a higher propensity for adults who lived with violence as children to have involvement with violent partners, this is a minority of all those who were maltreated as children (Dixon *et al.*, 2005).

Despite the overwhelming evidence for attention needed in the early years of children's lives, adolescence is also a critical period and one that receives far less attention. Adolescents can be seen as either troubled or troubling, without trying to understand the reasons behind either of these. Getting it right in the early years is of crucial importance and will of course impact on the life-course trajectory of all children and young people. But we do need to pay more attention to these other critical years and address the gaps in our knowledge base about these.

Conclusion

Approaching child maltreatment from a socio-ecological perspective can help us understand the multiple layers that impact on children from an individual level right through to the wider communities in which they live. The increasing focus on neurobiology and neurodevelopment provides compelling reason to act early, but this needs to be balanced with a less deterministic approach to the long-term consequences of abuse. At a family level, strong attachment relationships are essential for healthy development. At a community level, the effects of disadvantage and material deprivation can impact on the parenting environment, and this in turn can extend to the next generation and beyond.

CHAPTER 4

Causality and the interaction of risk factors

Introduction

This chapter provides evidence that there is no single known cause of child abuse. It also illustrates that, although child maltreatment and especially child physical abuse occur across socio-economic, religious, cultural, racial and ethnic groups, research now recognises a number of risk factors commonly associated with maltreatment. Evidence supports the view that child abuse arises from the interaction of multiple factors across various inter-locking domains: parent and caregiver factors; child and family factors; and environmental factors. However, it must be emphasised that, while certain risk factors often are present among families where maltreatment occurs, this does not mean that the presence of these factors will always result in child abuse and neglect. A greater understanding of these risk factors can help professionals working with children and families both to identify maltreatment and high risk families and to intervene appropriately.

Most parents love their children and do everything in their power to protect them from harm and ensure they have the best possible upbringing. Even before they are born, children require parents who will provide for their physical, social and emotional needs, through the expression of love, a sense of security and the provision of care. Children, especially when they are younger, depend on parents and family to provide the stability and security required to form meaningful attachments, and to grow and develop in ways that are positive. It is easy to become dislodged from this fact when focusing on high risk families, but it is an important tenet and one that provides a good starting point. Thus, while the overwhelming majority of parents want the very best for their children, sometimes they are either unable or unwilling to provide this.

AETIOLOGY OF ABUSE

No one single cause has been identified that explains the occurrence of all cases of physical abuse. The multi-factorial nature of physical abuse requires a more comprehensive amalgam of models and conceptual frameworks to account for the heterogeneous set of cases classified as physical abuse (Giardino and Giardino, 2010).

Circumstances that may give rise to the occurrence of a child's injury via physically abusive actions have been organised into a typology with the following five subtypes (Giardino and Giardino, 2010):

- caregiver's angry and uncontrolled disciplinary response to actual or perceived misconduct of the child;
- caregiver's psychological impairment, which causes resentment and rejection of the child by the caregiver and a perception of the child as different and provocative;
- child left in care of a babysitter who is abusive;
- caregiver's use of substances that disinhibit behaviour;
- caregiver's entanglement in a domestic abuse situation.

This typology describes commonly observed circumstances that may result in non-accidental injury to children; however, it does not shed light on why the circumstance can lead to a child's injury. A study exploring how social information processes offers some insight into the trigger for child abuse. Crouch et al. (2008) hypothesised that high risk parents possess pre-existing schema that increase the likelihood that they will process child-related information in a manner that increases the risk of hostile and/or aggressive behaviour. The study specifically examined how parents processed infant crying. Crying, particularly prolonged crying, is well recognised as stressful to a vast majority of parents and has been cited as a key trigger in physically abusive episodes, particularly in relation to shaking (Showers, 2001; Shepherd and Sampson, 2000). According to their model, high risk parents make more negative interpretations of ambiguous child cues and may be more inclined to interpret infants' cries (which are often unclear with regard to their meaning) in negative or hostile terms. While much more research is needed in this area, Crouch et al.'s (2008) study highlights the association between infant crying and parental hostility and negative attribution towards their child. It also suggests that the relationship between child physical abuse risk status and exposure to hostility-related cues are predictive of parental interpretations, feelings and behaviours in responding to their infant.

In the field of sexual abuse there is a well-known, four-factor explanatory model, postulated by Finkelhor (1991), that examines the complex and sequential interactions between sexual arousal, emotional congruence, blockage and disinhibition. As yet, there are no equivalent explanatory models for child physical abuse. A preliminary psychological typology of physical abuse based on personality characteristics appeared nearly twenty years ago (Francis *et al.*, 1992), but was extremely broad and does not appear to have been built on since. Although there are numerous theories regarding inter-generational transmission and more recent neuroscience discoveries and resilience models, there is a gap in our understanding of what is the most useful theoretical model for physical violence, and what information can be gleaned from this regarding effective inhibitors of physical abuse.

Gendered elements
Furthermore, while all forms of child abuse are perpetrated by both women and men, the nature and extent of male and female involvement are distinct and also vary across different types of abuse. For example, it is known that child sexual abuse is perpetrated mainly by men; while more women than men tend to be implicated in neglect – unsurprisingly given that women are the primary carers for children. There is currently very little systematic analysis of gender differences in the perpetration of physical abuse of children. There is unconfirmed information to suggest that, along the physical punishment/physical abuse continuum, women are more likely to be involved in physical punishment of children than men, while at the more serious end of the continuum men may be the more likely perpetrators of more serious physical abuse. There is a need to test this hypothesis to extend our understanding of child physical abuse.

IDENTIFYING ABUSED INFANTS

Across the UK there is a range of professionals who provide services to parents of infants. However, the international research literature indicates that non-reporting of child abuse concerns is a key issue, and there is evidence of fairly high levels of non-reporting across a range of different countries and professional disciplines (Wallace and Bunting, 2007). Although UK research examining this issue has been extremely limited, a survey of a thousand community nurses, general medical practitioners and general dental practitioners in Northern Ireland has shown non-reporting to be an issue (Lazenbatt and Freeman, 2006). The review by Professor Sir Ian Kennedy of National Health Services to children (Kennedy, 2010) made some damning observations, in particular with regard to: the low priority given to children; variability in thresholds for intervention; lack of cooperation between health and social services; and lack of attention to the early years (minus nine months to three years). There is a strong emphasis on providing Local Partnerships as part of the solutions.

The characteristics of the case, in particular the threshold of evidence available and the level of certainty this engenders in the reporter (Alvarez *et al.*, 2004), are central in determining if child abuse suspicions will be passed on, with emotional abuse and neglect being perceived as less serious and less likely to be reported as a result (Stokes and Schmidt, 2012). Reliance on physical evidence and victim disclosures only, and a reluctance to base decisions on interpretations of emotional and behavioural symptoms, also emerged as factors. Even in the presence of physical evidence and disclosures, a small group of 'diehard' non-reporters was identified and their lack of action linked with perceptions that reporting and legal interventions would only make matters worse for the child (Crenshaw *et al.*, 1995).

Analysis of the cases known to local authorities concluded that professionals sometimes became confused and uncertain about the significance of issues in complex and chaotic families, and that agencies tended to respond reactively to each situation as it arose, rather than seeing each in the context of the case history (Ofsted, 2010).

Research has also identified issues in diagnosing physical abuse in hospital settings. For example, a two-stage audit of 1,000 children presenting to an English hospital (Benger and Pearse, 2002) found that, in the first stage of the audit, adequate consideration of intentional injury were very limited, with only 2% of records explicitly documenting compatibility of history with injury and showing consistency of history. After the insertion of a reminder flowchart for assessing intentional injury, evidence that intentional injury had been considered increased to 70% of child hospital records and the number of children referred for further assessment increased from 0.6% to 1.4%. Anderst's (2008) American research has also shown that clinicians may not be using readily available, important information when considering the initiation of an abuse evaluation. NICE (2009) guidelines specifically stipulate that injuries to a child who is not independently mobile should trigger suspicions of physical abuse in the absence of an adequate explanation or alternative medical diagnosis. However, these guidelines have not been extended to Northern Ireland as yet, they are not applicable in Scotland and it is not known to what extent they are actually followed in the rest of the UK.

Risk factors and 'abusive' families

Parental low self-esteem, depression, psychopathology, history of child abuse and social isolation, among other factors, are at least somewhat steadily positively related to child maltreatment. Studies are also consistent in finding abusive parents: to be more psychophysiologically reactive to aversive child stimuli; to have unrealistic expectations of the child (either too high or too low); to use more coercive discipline than inductive reasoning; to have less interaction with the child; to be more negative than positive in interactions with the child; and to see the child as a problem child or as acting intentionally to annoy (Milner and Chilamkurti, 1991; Milner and Dopke, 1997). Social isolation also appears important (Hazler and Denham, 2002), while studies on parent substance abuse and child abuse suggest a positive relationship between the two, particularly in the case of alcohol abuse (Milner and Chilamkurti, 1991). None of the empirical literature reviews to date has cited demographic factors as particularly important in relation to child physical abuse, but important evidence is beginning to emerge from longitudinal studies.

Risk factors for child abuse (Black *et al.*, 2001)

Perpetrators:
- Few studies have investigated the fathers' characteristics.
- Only the association with parents' age had a medium-effect size.
- Parent gender is not associated with child abuse.
- Inter-generational transmission of abuse and a history of poor familial support were moderately associated with child physical abuse. Parents who were abused as children or corporally punished as teens were more likely to employ physical abuse, and abusive mothers also reported less family social support as children.
- Most personality variables assessed were not associated with child abuse.
- Abusive mothers were likely to make internal and stable attributions about their children's negative behaviours and external and unstable attributions about their children's positive behaviours; they were also less likely to blame themselves for failed interactions with their children. They also had more negative and higher than normal expectations of their children, as well as less understanding of appropriate developmental norms.
- Abusive mothers were more likely to use harsh discipline strategies and verbal aggression and less likely to use positive strategies than controls.

Victims:
- child gender is not a risk factor;
- attention deficits;
- internalising and externalising behaviours;
- socialised aggression.

Family:
- adolescents perceived their families as having higher levels of family stress and as being less adaptive and less cohesive;
- partner aggression;
- children from abusive families were observed emitting more negative commands towards fathers, negative physical behaviours towards family members, and possibly more negative behaviours towards their mothers.

Community:
- Drake and Pandey (1996) found that communities with greater poverty and a lower percentage of two-parent families had significantly higher rates of child abuse.

There are two meta-analyses in the literature that have assessed the risk factors associated with child abuse and have reported the related effect sizes. Black *et al.* (2001) broke down the effect sizes reported into perpetrator, victim, family and community risk factors (see box). A second meta-analysis of the literature (Stith *et al.*, 2009) determined the strength of the relationship between each risk factor and child abuse, using a socio-ecological model. Stith *et al.* sum up their study by pointing out that some less frequently studied factors (e.g. parent anger/hyper-reactivity, anxiety and psychopathology) are more strongly related to child abuse than other more studied variables (e.g. parent stress, parent social support and single parenthood). An exception to this is that parent perception of the child as a problem is frequently studied, as is the importance of parental experience of physical abuse and neglect. Although child misbehaviour is a popular topic of study relating to both child abuse and child neglect, maltreatment is more strongly associated with the perceptions of the parent regarding the child's behaviour than to other indicators of child behaviour.

The physical abuse of children has the richest risk factor research literature of any form of violence. A meta-analysis by Black *et al.*, (2001) sums this up well (see below).

Summary of meta-analysis of risk factors for physical abuse (Black *et al.*, 2001)

Child physical abuse has the richest risk factor research literature of any form of family violence. An etiological model based on moderate to strongly supported risk factors would begin with distal perpetrator variables of being abused as a child/teen and receiving less family social support as a child. Next might come current family variables such as parents' youth, father's drinking and families living in a community that is impoverished and/or has a lower percentage of two-parent families. More proximal variables that increase the probability of parents, especially mothers, employing severe or abusive physical tactics could include mothers' dysphoria (e.g. unhappiness, emotional distress, anxiety, loneliness and isolation, depression, somatic complaints, interpersonal problems, feelings of incompetence as a parent, a tendency toward becoming upset and angry), stress (more challenging life events, including single parenting and other family difficulties) and coping (most likely a protective factor, including problem solving and social support). Finally, risk factors that are proximal to abuse could include mothers' high reactivity (impulsivity, high negative affect and autonomic nervous system arousal), high risk parenting (harsh discipline strategies, verbal aggression, yelling) and negative attributions, as well as children's behaviour problems (e.g. socialised aggression, attention deficits and internalising and externalising behaviours).

Crouch *et al.* (2008) point out that the growing appreciation of the variability in outcomes for physically abused children has prompted attention towards factors that may serve as intervening variables. Probably, one of the most important factors is social support, traditionally regarded as a buffer that diminishes the detrimental effect of abuse (Litty *et al.*, 1996; Runtz and Schallow, 1997).

Only a very small proportion of children referred to social services become the subject of any formal child protection measures (Cleaver *et al.*, 2011). Based on an in-depth analysis of recent statistics, it is estimated that, for every child who is known to children's social services, another eight remain undetected and without help (Jütte *et al.*, 2013).

Predicting abuse
While it is helpful to understand risk factors, this is not the same as trying to develop actuarial tools that might help predict those families where physical abuse may occur. There are methodological, ethical and theoretical reasons why work on prediction is unhelpful (Taylor *et al.*, 2008; Munro *et al.*, 2014). We would prefer to suggest that such tools are not yet sufficiently discriminating, and that it is preferable to concentrate on adequate assessment of need (Daniel *et al.*, 2009). The presence of characteristics such as domestic abuse or mental illness does not predict serious abuse or death, but can increase the risk of harm to a child, creating a hazardous, frightening and chaotic environment (Brandon *et al.*, 2009). It is usually the accumulation of risk rather than the presence of any single risk factor that affects outcomes, and multiple risks are multiplicative rather than merely additive (Durlak, 1998).

Conclusion

Although our understanding of child abuse has advanced significantly over the last fifty years, there remain enormous gaps in our knowledge as to why abuse happens. There is certainly no single known cause, but rather it arises from the interaction of multiple factors. We have learnt much from studies into sexual abuse, but we know far less about physical abuse. We also do not yet fully understand the role of gender in abuse. And while certain risk factors are often present in families where abuse occurs, the presence of these does not mean abuse will always occur; and their absence does not mean that it will not. We have also some way to go in recognising abused children and young people. Making predictions about abuse is a zero-sum game, but we do need to get better at recognising and responding to children living in high risk families where multiple risk factors are present.

CHAPTER 5

Protective factors and resilience: increasing emotional well-being

Introduction

This chapter deals with the concepts of protective factors and resilience and how they can affect and increase childhood well-being, especially emotional well-being. In recent years there has been much focus on understanding the factors that help some children grow up to be healthy and well-functioning adults despite having to overcome various forms of adversity such as abuse and neglect. Such successful development under high risk conditions is known as resilience and much research (e.g. the Adverse Childhood Experiences (ACE) study) (Dube *et al.*, 2001) has been conducted on identifying protective factors and processes that might account for children's successful outcomes, especially their emotional well-being. The chapter further argues that there is no single path to resilience, because the risks and protective factors have diverse impacts at different developmental stages (Masten, 2012). Moreover, while some children may appear resilient in terms of their behaviour, it has been noted that they may still experience internal distress or suffer significant deficits in one aspect of life (e.g. emotional functioning), while displaying adaptive functioning in other aspects (e.g. academic achievement). The chapter concludes with a discussion of how supportive family functioning and good parenting can increase resilience and allow the development of emotional well-being.

> Resilience is the process of harnessing biological, psychosocial, structural, and cultural resources to sustain well-being (Panter-Brick and Leckman, 2013).

PROTECTIVE FACTORS, RESILIENCE AND EMOTIONAL WELL-BEING

The past twenty years of research have brought awareness to the vast individual differences in acute and long-term responses to childhood abuse and adversity. In some cases, children may not appear to exhibit significant effects from maltreatment (see Luthar and Zelazo, 2003; Collishaw *et al.*, 2007), as they have certain protective factors and resilience to negative consequences and have been buffered by personal characteristics such as optimism, high self-esteem or a sense of hopefulness despite their adverse circumstances. Evidence is continuing to be gathered which explores why certain children with composite risk factors and living in 'high risk' families become long-term victims, while other children with the same risks do not. The particular significance of multiple risks is also highlighted by the work of Sameroff *et al.* (1998) and Gutman *et al.* (2002), who found that, while there were significant effects of single risk factors, most children with only one risk factor were less likely to develop major problems.

The major risk factors for children tend to lie within chronic and transitional events, rather than in acute risks. Therefore, children show greater resilience when faced with acute adversities (e.g. bereavement or short-term illness) and less resilience when exposed to chronic risks (e.g. continuing parental conflict and violence, long-term poverty and multiple changes of home and school).

There are large individual variations in how children respond to adversity. Children appear to show greater resilience when faced with acute adversities and less resilience when exposed to chronic risks. However, Benard (2006) estimates that approximately half of children who experience multiple risks and adversities will overcome these and achieve relatively good outcomes. These children are often described as 'resilient'. However, considerable debate remains about the definition and assessment of this concept (Goldstein and Brooks, 2005). There are also individual differences in the timing of manifesting symptoms and the context in which children exhibit resilience: some individual children display few symptoms initially, but evidence 'sleeper' effects later in their development; other children appear resilient in one context but not in another (Li *et al.*, 2011).

Resilience refers to this process of positive adaptation despite exposure to significant adversity (Luthar, 2006; Masten, 2007). Recent research shows how resilience theory has shifted its focus of attention from efforts to appraise and understand risk or vulnerability in children, towards a more concentrated effort to enhance strength or capability in children. Although resilience may appear a simple concept, it is in fact often very difficult to operationalize, and given its multidimensional nature is best conceptualised across a range of outcomes (see Walsh *et al.*, 2010).

Although resilience is not always directly measured, it is now seen as a dynamic developmental process, rather than as a static trait. It has been defined as 'the potential to exhibit resourcefulness' (Pooley and Cohen, 2010) and 'adaptive capacities under conditions of environmental, stress or uncertainty' (Klohen, 1996). As Masten (2012) suggests: 'resilience is the capacity of a dynamic, malleable system to withstand challenges to its stability, viability or development.' Resilience is further defined as a term that describes the product of a combination of coping mechanisms in the context of adversity and is an important concept because it acknowledges each individual's unique developmental trajectory (Daniel *et al.*, 2009).

Resilience has also been found to have international relevance with cultural and context-specific characteristics (Ungar, 2008), including life-course variations (Hildan *et al.*, 2008). Resilience is therefore conceptualised as an outcome, as well as by a set of qualities that enable a person to make good use of internal and external resources (Wassell and Gilligan, 2010). Adding to the complexity of defining resilience, later developments in the literature present much crossover between resilience and concepts such as attachment, trauma, mental health and emotional well-being. In terms of the last concept, Mguni *et al.* (2012) argue that, while both resilience and emotional well-being are two sides of the same coin, they capture different points in time. Emotional well-being describes and captures a psychological state at one point in time, while resilience takes into account the past and the future, in that a person can build resilience before they hit a crisis (Mguni *et al.*, 2012).

Resilience is inferred from two component constructs: risk and positive adaptation (Luthar and Zelazo, 2003). Evidence shows that resilience can protect children who are in vulnerable and difficult situations doing this through the promotion of their sense of emotional well-being (Masten and Obradovic, 2006; Grant and Kinman, 2012), with linkages to emotional and social competencies (Kinman and Grant, 2011), positive emotions, optimism and hope (Collins, 2008) and hardiness and stress-resistant qualities (Beddoe *et al.,* 2011). Overall, the best evidence suggests that bolstering childhood protective factors such as resilience can be productive and allows children to enhance their emotional well-being resources. Importantly, resilient behaviours in children may be strengthened through reducing exposure to risk factors (e.g. child maltreatment and neglect, disadvantage and poverty, domestic violence, parental death, divorce and separation) and the promotion of protective factors (e.g. good attachment and security, parental mental well-being, educational achievement, self-efficacy and positive relationships with supportive adults and communities).

Resilience as a protective factor has been defined in increasingly complex ways towards highlighting multi-level interactions with environments and especially, the importance of available and accessible resources supporting adaptation (Supkoff *et al.,* 2012; Ungar, 2012; Cicchetti, 2014). Overall, the evidence suggests that these resilience and protective factors may reduce the negative consequences of risk factors through direct effects (compensatory model) or through interaction effects (risk-protective model – Fergus and Zimmerman, 2005). The compensatory model of resilience implies that protective factors can compensate for exposure to risk factors (Garmezy *et al.,* 1984; Masten and Wright, 1998), while the risk-protective model assumes that protective factors buffer or moderate the negative influence of exposure to risk or interact with risks to reduce their negative effect on children's outcomes (Rutter, 1985). Although there are obvious overlaps between the biomedical, psychological, social models (Shonkoff, 2010) and resilience-based models, no one theoretical model offers a complete understanding of all the issues involved, and resilient outcomes can result from dynamic transactions between developmental systems and environmental supports (Masten, 2007).

The study of resilience is therefore associated with human development, particularly those factors that enhance the experience of emotional well-being among children and young people who face significant adversity (Ungar, 2011; 2012). Following Bronfenbrenner's (1979) work, which moved theories of child development from individual to community/environment interactions, the study of resilience in children has also shifted conceptual thinking from a strong focus on the vulnerable child to the assessment of the social-ecological factors that facilitate the development of emotional well-being under stress (Ungar, 2011). This is both an important and powerful outlook as it suggests that resilience adds an extra dimension – that of future proofing to emotional well-being promotion and analysis. Emotional well-being is one of the most commonly used concepts to describe overall mental health and well-being for children and young people, and their later life outcomes (Love *et al.*, 2005). It is a key factor in the overall health and success of individuals and society as a whole (Layard *et al.*, 2005). Emotional well-being is a multifaceted concept, and can be used in conjunction with, and to some extent as interchangeable with, concepts such as emotional intelligence, emotional literacy and social and emotional competence (Mayer and Salovey, 1997). Increasingly, the concept of 'resilience' is being seen as an additional and useful indicator of overall well-being, and emotional well-being in particular. Children's effective use of their emotions enables them to control their reactions in stressful conditions, to learn to communicate their emotional state better, to develop healthy relationships with family and friends, and to become successful in school, work and life (Elias *et al.*, 1997).

There is also a range of other theoretical models that focus more on these positive assets and the resources needed to support vulnerable children. These include: general strengths approaches (Roehlkepartain and Sesma, 2007); salutogenesis (Antonovsky, 1996); social capital (Puttnam, 2000; Morris *et al.*, 2008); and emotional well-being (Masten and Obradovic, 2006), which looks at how children and young people manage stress and stay well. Rutter (2007) highlights three important considerations in the complexities involved in thinking about resilience and these overlap with some other theoretical models. He suggests that: overcoming cumulative risks may depend on childhood experiences before and after the trauma; children and young people may have different genetic and physical responses to adversity, which may account for some of the differences in outcome; and the mediating mechanisms that enable some people to be resilient to adversity may involve what they do in response. However, evidence clearly describes specific resource factors or assets that may have the potential to buffer or ameliorate the detrimental effects of adversity and lead to resilient outcomes. Wright and Masten (2005) argue that positive adaptational resources are helpful to the individual child regardless of exposure to risk or adversity, and that these protective factors can be a person or context, which also work as a process (e.g. the process of overcoming stress) or act as a buffering mechanism (e.g. good attachments) (Marriott *et al.*, 2014).

Examining these resources that appear to protect children from the risks of maltreatment is vitally important, yet protective factors have not been studied as extensively as risk factors. Luthar and Zelazo (2003) group these factors into three socio-ecological domains (Bronfenbrenner and Morris, 1998).

- children's internal characteristics and strengths, e.g., self-esteem, self-efficacy, self-control;
- family characteristics and relationships, e.g., child–parent closeness, parenting styles;
- characteristics of children's social (particularly school) environment, e.g., student–teacher relationships, school quality.

Research further suggests that a supportive family environment (e.g., two-parent households, high parental education) and social support are two protective factors (Kotch *et al.*, 1999). It is also the quality of the parent–infant relationship in particular that will create the conditions for establishing healthy patterns of social and emotional functioning (Stein *et al.*, 1991; Murray *et al.*, 1996). There is some very good evidence to show that parent resilience and having stable extended family units and living in communities with strong social cohesion can be very powerfully protective, even in the face of other adversities (Butchart *et al.*, 2006). As stated earlier in this book, research has shown that 'good' parenting is influenced by the parents' mental health and that mental-health problems such as maternal postnatal depression can interfere with positive parenting, having a long-term effect on children's socio-emotional development, particularly in the case of boys (Murray *et al.*, 1996). A systematic review by Moran *et al.* (2004) shows that a variety of parent support programmes such as *What Works in Parenting Support?* can be effective in promoting the sort of parenting that improves children's social and emotional development. Their findings suggest that:

> ... provision of parenting programmes still represents an important pathway to helping parents, especially when combined with local and national policies that address the broader contextual issues that affect parents' and children's lives (Moran *et al.*, 2004).

Indeed, resilience can be defined as 'normal development under difficult conditions' (Fonagy *et al.*, 1994). So, in the same way that there are factors that increase susceptibility of children and families to abuse, there are also factors that may offer protective effects (Butchart *et al.*, 2006). In their workbooks on assessing and promoting resilience in vulnerable children, Daniel and Wassell (2002a; 2002b; 2002c) describe the protective factors that might explain why some children seem to fare better in adverse circumstances than others. The level of resilience can be seen as falling on a dimension of resilience and vulnerability. This dimension tends to focus on intrinsic qualities of an individual (e.g. an 'easy' temperament is associated with resilience in infancy). Another dimension for the understanding of individual differences is that of protective and adverse environments. This dimension concerns extrinsic factors, such as wider family support. When these dimensions are considered together, they provide a useful framework for assessment and is being used widely in Scotland (Scottish Government, 2008).

Cicchetti (2013) consider more natural and genetically applied adaptation processes (see review by Wu *et al.*, 2013), which implies a neuroscience of resilience, founded on the principle of plasticity. Future developments in this field will be interesting to watch.

In their review of research on child maltreatment and resilience, Afifi and MacMillan (2011) highlight that resilience changes over time and developmental phases. Resilience can therefore be seen as a complex issue following the socio-ecological models of development and each child needs to be assessed on an individual basis (Daniel and Wassell, 2002a). The resilience matrix can help plot out those factors that need strengthening as well as those that should be further supported (Scottish Government, 2008). Research by Butchart *et al.* (2006) and Durlak (1998) has indicated clearly that the factors that appear to facilitate resilience include:

- secure attachment of the infant to an adult caregiver;
- high levels of paternal presence and care during childhood (Resnick *et al.*, 2004);
- lack of association with antisocial, criminal or substance-abusing peers (Resnick *et al.*, 2004);
- a warm and supportive relationship with a non-offending parent (Farrell *et al.*, 2010; Resnick *et al.*, 2004);
- a lack of abuse-related stress;
- intelligence;
- capacity for emotional regulation;
- school achievement and connectedness to school (Cedeno *et al.*, 2010);
- clear boundaries, with positive, non-physical discipline techniques;
- access to mental-health services (see Gask *et al.*, 2012; Conrod *et al.*, 2013);
- close relationship networks (e.g. see reviews by Allen, 2011a; Herman *et al.*, 2011; Afifi and MacMillan, 2011; Cicchetti, 2013);
- effective social policies.

Conclusion

This chapter discussed the recent movements in the field of resilience research, which have emphasised taking a developmental and lifespan approach to examining the protective factors associated with good or better outcomes for children and young people with histories of mal-treatment, as little is known about the factors that contribute to long-term resilience. We drew attention to protective factors that provide positive assets or resources, rather than those models focused solely on addressing deficits offers and showed many promising avenues for future research and intervention. However, effective and efficient assessment and having a range of treatment options are the keys to future success.

CHAPTER 6

Effective prevention and treatment interventions

Introduction

> Early intervention is needed to make lasting improvements in the
> lives of our children, to forestall many persistent social problems
> and end their transmission from one generation to the next, and to
> make long-term savings in public spending (Allen, 2011a, p. viii).

As discussed in the introductory chapter, the high personal and public
costs of child maltreatment make identification through effective early
prevention programmes a high policy, practice and research priority. This final chapter brings together the evidence that highlights the
extensive efforts to prevent and treat child maltreatment and shows
how these have expanded considerably over the past three decades.
We debate the use and effectiveness of a variety of approaches to
prevent child abuse and neglect, including parent education, home
visitation and several community-wide programmes. Home visiting is
highlighted as one of the most popular approaches in preventing child
maltreatment, and is the most cited for its potential. However, the chapter stresses that, although some promising maltreatment prevention
strategies have been identified, research continues to suffer from a
number of methodological limitations, thus limiting the knowledge of
how prevention programmes impact on different forms of child abuse
and neglect.

Again, as emphasised earlier, child maltreatment is a global public
health and social problem and its prevalence translates into a significant economic burden to society, cutting across many different service
sectors including child welfare, health and mental care, special education and criminal justice (Dozier *et al.,* 2006; 2008). The major consensus from research is that child maltreatment has a significant impact on
multiple and overlapping areas of development, beginning for the infant
and child when the first trauma begins, and unless protective factors

or intervention are in operation the effects may become long-term, into adulthood and beyond (Cicchetti, 2014). These serious adverse consequences of childhood abuse and neglect can lead to longer-term emotional and mental-health problems, delinquency and violent behaviour and chronic disorders.

Across health and social service sectors, public health departments are responsible for identifying or developing primary prevention interventions or programmes to address these core public health issues at a population health level. However, the challenge is that each specific category of child maltreatment is often associated with unique but sometimes overlapping risk indicators that require abuse-specific interventions and prevention programmes. For example, the most common negative effects of sexual abuse in childhood manifest in emotional and behavioural problems, post-traumatic stress symptoms, depression, suicidal ideation and self-harm behaviours, anxiety, substance abuse, aggression, self-esteem issues, academic problems and sexualised behaviours (Marriott *et al.*, 2014). Emotional abuse can have a severe impact on a developing child's mental health and well-being, behaviour and self-esteem, particularly when it occurs in infancy. Thus, underlying emotional abuse may be as important, if not more so, than other, more visible forms of abuse, in terms of its impact on the child (Jordan and Sketchley, 2009).

METHODOLOGICAL ISSUES

Increased recognition of the consequences associated with child maltreatment has led to greater emphasis on its prevention. With this in mind, there is immediate need for improving and building the evidence base for interventions to promote the well-being of maltreated children and prevent many longer-term consequences. However, a central and ongoing barrier to conducting rigorous research appears to be the employment of randomisation or quasi-randomisation procedures. Although promising maltreatment prevention strategies have been identified, research continues to suffer from methodological limitations and a narrow focus on select prevention models.

As summarised in several reviews (e.g. Sweet and Appelbaum, 2004; Geeraert *et al.*, 2004; Klevens and Whitaker, 2007; MacMillan *et al.*, 2008; Mikton and Butchart, 2009; Reynolds *et al.*, 2009), maltreatment prevention initiatives have often targeted expectant primiparous mothers and families with young infants and children.

For example, in a review of child maltreatment interventions, only one parenting programme was identified as effective at preventing the recurrence of physical abuse, and no interventions were identified as stopping the recurrence of neglect (MacMillan *et al.*, 2008). Meanwhile, a small number of interventions resulted in improved behavioural or mental-health outcomes in children who had been neglected, exposed to intimate partner violence or sexually abused (Thacker and Stroup 1998).

Overall, most evaluations of maltreatment prevention initiatives have suffered from significant methodological limitations, and there is a striking lack of empirically and theoretically sound evaluation of interventions, with many studies now dated (Corcoran, 2000). Maltreatment intervention research, particularly comparative research, remains a relatively emerging field, with much of the work relying on small samples and having limited statistical power, so data cannot be stratified based on subgroups or considered in terms of potential mediators and moderators of effect. Indeed, only one exploratory study has examined mediating paths leading from participation in an early childhood intervention to reduced maltreatment (Reynolds and Robertson, 2003).

A further major methodological gap in the literature with implications for widespread implementation is the issue of 'dose' or how much of an intervention is needed to affect change in children and for what period of time this works. Also, the definition of maltreatment presented throughout studies is a major challenge, with many of these defining maltreatment in terms of a child's involvement with the Crown Prosecution Service (CPS) or substantiation of alleged abuse.

The use of common and validated measures for identifying symptoms to define clinical and social need is also a major omission, undermining the strength of the evidence base. A systematic review highlights these inconsistencies in measurements and definition of child maltreatment to illustrate the importance of and need for international efforts to standardise studies to enhance the comparability of findings (Norman *et al.*, 2012).

Most importantly, there is limited knowledge of how prevention programmes impact on different forms of maltreatment, and there is a dearth of interventions that demonstrate impacts on child neglect (DePanfilis and Dubowitz, 2005; Mersky *et al.*, 2009). For example, Randomised Control Trials (RCTs) should recognise the fact that limiting inclusion in a clinical trial to a single subtype of maltreatment is potentially problematic, as we know that the majority of maltreated children experience multiple forms of mal-treatment such as physical abuse and neglect. Children are known to live in 'high risk' environments, where they suffer interacting abuse from parental domestic violence, alcohol abuse and mental-health issues. As Toth *et al.* (2013) suggest: 'To engage the "real world" maltreatment client effectively, sufficient resources need to be available to the research to support the challenges in recruit-ing and retaining a population that is routinely confronted with multiple problems.' There is therefore a need for increased research investment in studies that represent the complexities in the lives of maltreated children and their families.

Key issues for research methodologies
- Definition of maltreatment needs strengthening and internationally operationalised;
- validated measures needed to identify symptoms to define clinical and social need;
- international efforts to standardise studies to enhance the comparability of findings;
- all studies showed high attrition rates;
- more research needed with large samples to provide statistical power;
- knowledge of how prevention programmes impact on different forms of maltreatment;
- more research needed on how to retain participants for the whole duration of treatment;
- researchers need to include practitioners in the evaluations;
- recognition of potential mediator and moderator effects;
- 'dose' and timing components recognised and evaluated;
- some programmes targeted factors that are not identified as known risk factors (e.g. poor early bonding, knowledge of child abuse);
- some factors were highly popular among programmes (e.g.

social isolation, parenting knowledge, access to services);
- highly prevalent risk factors have been neglected;
- there have been very limited efforts to modify other risk factors (e.g. teenage pregnancy, cognitive inflexibility, social skills deficits, harsh discipline, family conflict, poverty);
- programmes delivered by or to the public and requiring least effort were found to be most effective, however evaluation of programmes was difficult;
- poverty and partner violence (with focus on the children) as risk factors have been neglected;
- more research needed on teenage parenthood;
- surveillance bias is problematic among many studies;
- there is evidence that supports further investigation of flexible, multimodal and ecologically based interventions;
- many of the interventions have been adapted for UK;
- most studies focus on high risk groups;
- observed improvements in parent–child interactions may not mirror real life interactions;
- difficult to measure success in child maltreatment prevention.

Central to family and child welfare policy is a focus on effective and efficient prevention and early intervention. The publication of Graham Allen and Iain Duncan-Smith's report on early intervention in 2008 brought these to the fore (Allen and Duncan-Smith, 2008). Drawing on more recent research reviews and policy documents, the Centre for Social Justice (2011, p. 2) suggests that an effective framework for early intervention would comprise the following five components:
- a commitment to prevention;
- priority focus on the early years;
- continuing early intervention in later years;
- multi-agency systems approach;
- high quality of workforce.

The early years of life are now seen as a critical period when infants and children are making socio-emotional attachments and forming the crucial first relationships, which lay the foundations for future emotional and mental health (Fonagy *et al.*, 2002b;

Schore, 2010). All types of maltreatment can affect a child's emotional, psychological and mental well-being. The immediate and longer-term impact of abuse can include anxiety, irritability and eating disorders (Belsky *et al.*, 2010). Longitudinal and retrospective studies link disorganised emotional attachment in childhood, as a consequence of abuse and neglect, to a number of severe mental-health problems in adulthood, such as depression, severe anxiety, addictions, drug and alcohol abuse, PTSD, self-harming and suicide, as well as being bullied (MacMillan *et al.*, 2008). Infants who experience rejection or neglect are more likely to develop anti-social traits as they grow up and are more associated with borderline personality disorders and violent behaviour (Kendall-Tackett, 2003). Much earlier interventions for maltreatment had focused almost exclusively on parenting, hoping that, if the maltreatment could be ended or improved through more effective parenting, then adverse consequences could be abated. However, evidence now tells us that these types of interventions may not always support children through more positive trajectories (Toth *et al.*, 2013).

There is a strong evidence base that parenting interventions are effective in reducing harsh parenting, improving positive parenting skills and reducing child problem behaviour. Family-focused interventions may aim both to prevent recurrence of abuse and ensure better outcomes for the child, because they concentrate on the interactions between all family members as well as the mental health of each member (Carr, 2009). There is a relatively limited evidence base in this area, but these interventions are often used in practice with families presenting with multiple problems including child maltreatment. Parenting programmes, particularly those that are group based, are increasingly being recognised as being a cost-effective way of intervening to improve parenting (NICE, 2006), and to provide parents with access to other sources of peer-based support. Overall, while the evidence is inconclusive, there are few other interventions that have better established levels of empirical support as regards intervening with physically abusive parents.

Although promising approaches to preventing the maltreatment of young children have begun to emerge, as stated earlier lingering gaps in the literature remain. Recent reviews (MacMillan, 2009;

MacMillan *et al.*, 2009; Mikton and Butchart, 2009; Reynolds *et al.*, 2009; Selph *et al.*, 2013) have identified a few rigorously evaluated, promising approaches, but programme effects have been inconsistent on replication and difficult to take to scale. Of the early childhood interventions that have been cited for their potential to prevent maltreatment, home visitation manualised models have received the most attention (see Bilukha *et al.*, 2005; Howard and Brooks-Gunn, 2009, for reviews). To a lesser extent, parent education programmes and school-based, sexual abuse prevention programmes (Mikton and Butchart, 2009) have been adopted for evaluation. A systematic review of parenting interventions identified complex, multifaceted home visitation programmes targeting at-risk families as effective at preventing unintentional injuries in children – a proxy measure of neglect (Kendrick *et al.*, 2007). Three recent integrative reviews identified the Nurse-Family Partnership (NFP) programme with nurses frequently visiting targeted young, low-income, first-time mothers from pregnancy (less than twenty-nine weeks gestation) until the child is two years of age, as demonstrating the best evidence with multiple consistent and enduring beneficial maternal and child health outcomes; they are seen as the best available means of preventing child maltreatment (Kitzman *et al.*, 1997; Olds *et al.*, 2002; MacMillan *et al.*, 2009). Overall children of young mothers who participated in the programme were significantly less likely to have been victims of substantiated maltreatment than control children (Cicchetti and Toth, 2005).

The NFP is consistently identified as having higher benefit-to-cost ratios per participant than most other prevention programmes for parents of infants and young children in the United States Krugman et al 2007). Subsequent investigations of the NFP and other home visitation interventions have yielded mixed results with respect to maltreatment and related outcomes. For example, the Triple P – Positive Parenting Program – has shown positive effects on maltreatment and associated outcomes, but further assessment and replication are needed (MacMillan *et al.*, 2009). Moreover, hospital-based educational programmes to prevent abusive head trauma in infants and children at risk of physical abuse and neglect show promise but also require further assessment.

There have been a number of helpful systematic reviews that shed light on child abuse. These include those that have examined:

- research done in the ten years following the Adoption and Safe Families Act 1997 (ASFA) on effectiveness of treatment for families with physical abuse (Oliver and Washington, 2009). The Act limits the time a child can spend in care (no more than fifteen out of twenty-two months) – otherwise parental rights to the child will be ended – making it paramount that social workers have access to efficient treatment programmes and bringing the children home fast and safe;
- family interventions with parents who had abused and/or neglected their children (Corcoran, 2000);
- primary prevention programmes of child abuse and neglect, in order to identify gaps and future directions from a public health perspective (Klevens and Whitaker, 2007);
- reviews on the interventions to prevent or ameliorate child physical abuse and neglect (Barlow *et al.*, 2007);
- primary prevention of child abuse and neglect; representative outcomes were hospitalisation, rates of visitation to emergency rooms and injury rates (MacMillan *et al.*, 1994);
- effective interventions for children and families where a child has experienced physical abuse (Montgomery *et al.*, 2009);
- approaches to reduce the five major subtypes of child maltreatment (physical abuse, sexual abuse, psychological abuse, neglect and exposure to intimate-partner violence) and the impairment associated with these experiences (MacMillan *et al.*, 2009);
- effectiveness of parenting programmes, which were defined as standardised interventions that are delivered to parents with the aim of changing parenting attitudes and practices, improving parenting skills, reducing parenting stress, improving maternal psychosocial functioning, improving family dynamics or reducing child behavioural problems (Barlow *et al.*, 2008).

All of these reviews have fairly consistent results and overall can be summarised thus:

- engaging children and/or the whole family in treatment is gaining in popularity;
- it seems to be important to address parental social needs;
- more focus on parental psychological needs is needed;
- there are low numbers of male caregivers;
- parents minimise problems at home, making it difficult to determine the effectiveness of interventions;
- abusive parents tend to attribute negative connotations to the children's behaviour and expect children to perform at a higher level than they are capable of, which can escalate into violence (mostly physical abuse);
- more fathers/male carers need to be included in the treatment process;
- more attention should be given to substance abuse treatment;
- families at risk should be offered preventative home-visiting services early in the baby's life.

Interventions for child abuse: key messages

- The most consistent and promising evidence supported the effectiveness of parenting interventions such as Webster-Stratton's Incredible Years and Parent-Child Interaction Therapy for improving parent-child interactions and child mental-health outcomes (Webster-Stratton, 1990).
- Cognitive behavioural therapy (CBT) demonstrates positive results with abusive parents, but has a narrow focus on individual cognition.
- Home-visiting programmes demonstrate a small to moderate overall impact and similar size impact to abuse reduction.
- Parenting programmes have an overall moderate effect – larger results being obtained post intervention than at follow-ups.
- Home-visiting programmes and parenting programmes are associated with savings.
- Although many interventions did not show a reduction of child maltreatment, evidence does indicate that extended home visitation can prevent physical abuse and neglect in disadvantaged families.
- Family therapy is controversial, implying that both perpetrator and victim are connected in a circular and reciprocal way. Family therapy may be effective for improving parental discipline, reducing parent–child conflict, and child abuse potential.
- Increasing social support for families is shown to be important. The

families who received this intervention improved, compared with those who did not, but their improvement was not enough to prevent the risk of maltreatment.

- A-theoretical treatments (i.e. no theory ones, e.g. stress management, marital counselling, therapeutic day care), usually for parents with very young children, are generally positive but difficult to measure.
- The effectiveness of home visiting is shown only in high risk populations and cannot guarantee success in the general population.
- Intensive short-term, home-based support for families whose children are at risk for out-of-home placement show overall improvement.
- No evidence of effectiveness for media-based interventions.
- Early preventative interventions can be helpful: for example, family support, preschool education/childcare and community development. Some of these were moderately effective (hospital-based perinatal programmes, perinatal coaching and home visiting and agency counselling), while others (perinatal coaching with support group and support groups alone) were ineffective.
- Many interventions such as family preservation services, home visiting, psychodrama, therapeutic day treatment, individual child psychotherapy and art therapy do not have sufficient evidence to support their effectiveness because of a lack of well-conducted studies and limited outcome measures.
- Residential treatment and play therapy were not found to be effective.

Some particular interventions have demonstrated effectiveness.

Nurse–family partnerships, USA

Nurses provide home visitation to low-income, first-time mothers, beginning prenatally and continuing during infancy. The first and second NFP trials included an additional treatment condition of prenatal visitation without the intensive postpartum component. The group receiving prenatal and intensive postnatal intervention showed the most positive outcomes. The NFP has undergone the most rigorous and extensive evaluation of child maltreatment outcomes. It has been tested, with high rates of retention, in three RCTs across a range of samples and US regions.

Early Start programme, New Zealand

This programme is an intensive home-visiting programme targeted at families facing stress and difficulties (Fergusson et al, 2012). At age three, children had significantly lower attendance rates at hospital for childhood injuries than the control group, and fewer admissions to hospital for severe abuse and neglect. Early Start children had about a third of the rate of parent-reported physical abuse. However, rates of referral to official agencies for care and protection concerns were similar for Early Start children and those in the control group. This apparent lack of difference was attributed to the fact that Early Start clients were under closer surveillance and hence more likely to be referred to official agencies than those in the control group.

Abusive head trauma education programmes
The most widely adopted prevention strategy in US hospitals aims to stop abusive head trauma (shaken impact syndrome, as SBS is known in the USA). An educational intervention (leaflet, video, posters) about the dangers of infant shaking and ways to handle persistent crying was provided to parents in sixteen hospitals in New York State. The incidence of abusive head trauma was substantially reduced during the sixty-six months after introduction of the programme compared with the sixty-six months before the study (Wyszynski, 1999).

Enhanced paediatric care for families at risk
The Safe Environment for Every Kid (SEEK) model of paediatric primary care in a continuity clinic in Baltimore, MD, USA demonstrated a number of benefits, including apparently fewer child-protection services reports, fewer instances of medical neglect and less harsh punishment reported by parents (Dubowitz et al., 2011). Although this study had modest effects on reports to child-protection services, the results suggest that enhancing physicians' abilities to help families decrease risk factors for child maltreatment could be effective.

Parent-training programmes
Parent-training programmes have been included in several reviews of interventions for physically abusive parents (MacLeod and Nelson, 2000; Edgeworth and Carr, 2000), but only one had focused explicitly

on the effectiveness of training programmes for physically abusive and neglectful parents (Barlow *et al.*, 2008). This review reported little evidence to support the use of parent-training programmes to reduce the recurrence of physical abuse. The most effective type of programme seems to be the Parent-Child Interaction Therapy (PCIT). There is also evidence to suggest that some types of parenting programmes could be effective in improving some outcomes that are associated with physically abusive parenting, including, for example, child reports of parental anger.

Disadvantaged communities

Promising results have been shown in various programmes run within community settings, such as the Perry Preschool Program, Project 12-Ways, the US Head Start programs (Lutzker and Rice, 1984) and a number of other programmes that provide a variety of support to mothers and children from disadvantaged communities (McDowell and Lyons, 2009). Evaluations of Sure Start in the UK also report provision of an improved learning environment at home and the increase in use of support services by families (Melhuish *et al.*, 2008).

If there are no rigorously evaluated effective interventions, public health researchers can build on identified risk and protective factors and on established theoretical models to develop and test primary prevention interventions. Mrazek and Haggerty (1994) developed a comprehensive framework that many consider the 'gold standard' for guiding the development of such interventions. This framework complements the steps of the public health approach and includes five fundamental stages:

- problem identification and measurement;
- identification of risk and protective factors and theoretical models from multiple fields;
- intervention development, training of interveners and conduct of small-scale pilot or feasibility studies leading to an RCT that replicates the intervention;
- conduct of large-scale RCT to establish effectiveness;
- broad implementation of the intervention and ongoing programme evaluation.

While there is promise in a number of interventions, it is not always possible to draw inferences specifically for child abuse. Studies that have incorporated measures of the incidence of child abuse provide no evidence to support the use of parenting programmes to treat abuse. However, there is limited evidence that some parenting programmes may be effective in improving some outcomes that are associated with physically abusive parenting. There is also limited evidence to suggest that programmes that provide additional components aimed specifically at addressing factors associated with physically abusive parenting, such as anger and stress, may be more effective when compared with parenting programmes that do not include such components. The available evidence points to the potential value of programmes that are based on approaches such as CBT and child-parent interaction therapy. Other well-recognised interventions such as the Webster-Stratton (1990) programme also appear to have a role in treating outcomes that are associated with abusive parenting. While behavioural child management programmes appear to have some benefit, they may need to be more broadly focused to secure improvements in other aspects of parenting, such as positive child affect.

Issues for research

- All studies showed high attrition rates.
- More research is needed with large samples.
- More research required on how to retain participants for the whole duration of treatment.
- Researchers should include practitioners in the evaluations.
- Some programmes targeted factors that are not identified as known risk factors (e.g. poor early bonding, knowledge of child abuse).
- Some factors were highly popular among programmes (e.g. social isolation, parenting knowledge, access to services).
- Highly prevalent risk factors have been neglected.
- There have been very limited efforts to modify other risk factors (e.g. teenage pregnancy, cognitive inflexibility, social skills deficits, harsh discipline, family conflict, poverty).
- Programmes delivered by or to the public and requiring least effort were found to be most effective; however, evaluation of programmes was difficult.

- Poverty and partner violence (with focus on children) as risk factors have been neglected.
- More research should be done on teenage parenthood.
- Surveillance bias was problematic among many studies.
- There is evidence that supports further investigation of flexible, multimodal and ecologically based interventions.
- Many of the interventions have been adapted for the UK.
- Most studies focused on high risk groups.
- Observed improvements in parent–child interactions may not mirror real life interactions.
- It is difficult to measure success in child maltreatment prevention.

There is a strong evidence base that parenting interventions are effective in reducing harsh parenting, improving positive parenting skills and decreasing child problem behaviour. Family-focused interventions may aim to prevent recurrence of abuse and to ensure better outcomes for the child because they concentrate on the interactions between all family members as well as on the mental health of each member (Carr, 2009). There is a relatively limited evidence base in this area, but these interventions are often used in practice with families presenting with multiple problems including child maltreatment.

Parenting programmes, particularly those that are group based, are increasingly being recognised as being a cost-effective way of intervening to improve parenting (NICE, 2006) and to provide parents with access to other sources of peer-based support. Overall, while the evidence is inconclusive, there are few other interventions that have better established levels of empirical support as regards intervening with physically abusive parents.

IMPLEMENTATION AND EVALUATION OF EVIDENCE-BASED INTERVENTIONS AND POLICIES

Future research should pay heightened attention to the consistent use of measures with well-established validity, particularly assessment of improvement in the parent–child relationship. A paradigm shift is required on the part of researchers and funders alike, to galvanise the commitment and resources necessary for conducting collaborative, clinical, multisite trials with these particularly vulnerable children and families. There is a pressing need, especially when resources are limited, for all public health departments to implement effective interventions for high risk families, rather than providing programmes that have not been proved adequate or sufficient. The NFP programme is internationally recognised as the intervention most capable of preventing child maltreatment. Widely implemented across the United States, this innovative programme is currently being evaluated and replicated in England, Scotland, Germany, the Netherlands and Australia.

Conclusion

Child maltreatment remains a contemporary topic of concern and attention, but it needs to be refocused and reinvigorated. The interplay of the elements of the 'toxic trio' (domestic abuse, substance misuse and parental mental ill health) is critical. However, they are not the only risk factors for maltreatment and we need to retain focus on other risk factors and manifestations as well. There is an imbalance of research on the relative weightings of risk factors. For example, we do know much about the harms caused by domestic abuse experience, but we understand relatively little about social isolation. It could, ostensibly, be just as potent, but we have not yet looked at social isolation and psychological harm in as much depth.

Multiple risks have exponential and multiplicative effects; however, they are not additive. We do not know enough about the most toxic combinations of risk factors or in which circumstances these can be moderated. While the presence of certain characteristics cannot predict harm, it can increase the risk of harm. More work is needed on determining a typology of antecedents and determinants of maltreatment in high risk families. Engaging with children is crucial, but their voice is often lost. We have a central role to play in respecting a children's rights approach and making their voices heard.

Enhancing the prospects for healthy development in the lives of maltreated children therefore requires attention to enhancing opportunities for positive, non-violent family and peer interactions. As there are strong associations between child maltreatment and parental mental-health conditions or substance misuse and violence, there is a need for multi-professionals to consider the welfare of infants and children when dealing with these problems in adults. Also, as the needs of families are often multifaceted and interconnected, effective inter-agency and multi-professional response is crucial, with the main focus being on primary prevention in the early years. Improving the context of children's and families' lives (e.g. in relation to inequalities and housing, good-quality childcare, the benefits system and specialist substance misuse, mental health and domestic violence services) has the potential to reduce the likelihood of children suffering health and mental-health consequences of maltreatment. However, despite the magnitude of the problem and increasing awareness of its high social and public health costs, preventing child maltreatment is not a political priority in most countries throughout the world. It is imperative that epidemiology and public health approaches work together at the forefront of national and international efforts to understand and prevent child maltreatment (Butchart, 2008). Child protection framed by and accountable to these public health imperatives would promote the short- and long-term well-being, health and development of all children, thus making child protection a community issue.

REFERENCES

Advisory Council on the Misuse of Drugs (2003) *Hidden Harm. Responding to the Needs of Children of Problem Drug Users: The Report of an Inquiry*, London: Advisory Council on the Misuse of Drugs (ACMD)

Advisory Council on the Misuse of Drugs (2007) *Hidden Harm – Update*, London: Advisory Council on the Misuse of Drugs (ACMD)

Afifi, T. O. and MacMillan, H. L. (2011) 'Resilience following child maltreatment: a review of protective factors', *Canadian Journal of Psychiatry*, Vol. 56, pp. 266–72

Ainsworth, M. D., Blehar, M. C., Waters, E. and Wall, S. (1978) *Patterns of Attachment*, Hillsdale, NJ: Lawrence Erlbaum Associates

Ainsworth, M. D. (1979) 'Infant-mother attachment', *American Psychologist*, Vol. 34, pp. 932–7

Aldridge, J. (2006) 'The experiences of children living with and caring for parents with mental illness', *Child Abuse Review*, Vol. 15, pp. 79–88

Allen, B. (2011a) 'The use and abuse of attachment theory in clinical practice with maltreated children, part 1: diagnosis and assessment', Trauma, *Violence and Abuse*, Vol. 12, pp. 3–12

Allen, B. (2011b) 'Utilization and implementation of trauma-focused cognitive-behavioural therapy for the treatment of maltreated children', *Child Maltreatment*, Vol. 13, pp. 1–6

Allen, G. and Duncan-Smith, I. (2008*) Early Intervention: Good Parents, Great Kids, Better Citizens*, London: Centre for Social Justice and the Smith Institute. Available from URL: www.centreforsocialjustice.org.uk/publications/early-intervention-good-parents-great-kids-better-citizens (accessed 21 July 2014)

Altepeter, T. S. and Walker, C. E. (1992) 'Prevention of physical abuse of children through parent training', in Willis, D. J., Holden, E. W. and Rosenberg, M. S. (eds) (1992) *Prevention of Child Maltreatment: Developmental and Ecological Perspectives*, New York, NY: Wiley

Alvarez, K. M., Kenny, M. C., Donohue, B. and Carpin, K. M. (2004) 'Why are professionals failing to initiate mandated reports of child maltreatment, and are there any empirically based training programs to assist professionals in the reporting process?', *Aggression and Violent Behavior*, Vol. 9, pp. 563–78

American Academy of Pediatrics Committee on Child Abuse and Neglect and Committee on Community Health Services (1999) 'Investigation and review of unexpected infant and child deaths', *Journal of Pediatrics*, Vol. 104, pp. 1158–60

American Psychiatric Association (2011) *Diagnostic and Statistical Manual of*

Mental Disorders, New York: APA

Anda, R. and Brown, D. (2010) 'Adverse childhood experiences and population health', in *Washington: The Face of a Chronic Public Health Disaster*, Albany, NY: Family Policy Council

Anda, R., Felitti, V., Brown, D. *et al.* (2006) 'Insights into intimate partner violence from the Adverse Childhood Experiences (ACE) study', in Salber, P. and Taliaferro, E. (eds) (2006) *The Physician's Guide to Intimate Partner Violence and Abuse*, Volcano, CA: Volcano Press, pp. 77–88

Anderst, J. (2008) 'Assessment of factors resulting in abuse evaluations in young children with minor head trauma', *Child Abuse & Neglect*, Vol. 32, pp. 405–13

Angst, J., Gamma, A. and Roessler, W. (2011) 'Childhood adversity and chronicity of mood disorders', *European Archives of Psychiatry and Clinical Neuroscience*, Vol. 261, pp. 21–7

Anooshian, F. (2005) 'Violence and aggression in the lives of homeless children', *Aggression and Violent Behaviour*, Vol. 10, pp. 129–52

Antonovsky, A. (1996) 'The salutogenic model as a theory to guide health promotion', *Health Promotion International*, Vol. 11, No. 1. pp. 11–18

Appel, A. E. and Holden, G. W. (1998) 'The co-occurrence of spouse and physical child abuse: a review and appraisal', *Journal of Family Psychology*, Vol. 12, pp. 578–99

Bacchus, R. G. and Bewley, S. (2002) 'Women's perceptions and experiences of routine enquiry for domestic violence in a maternity service', *British Journal of Obstetrics and Gynaecology*, Vol. 109, pp. 9–16

Bagshaw, D., Chung, D., Couch, M., Lilburn, S. and Wadham, B. (2000) *Reshaping Responses to Domestic Violence*, Adelaide, SA: University of South Australia

Bair-Merritt, M. H., Blackstone, M. and Feudtner, C. (2006) 'Physical health outcomes of childhood exposure to intimate partner violence: a systematic review', *Paediatrics*, Vol. 2, p. 117

Balbernie, R. (2003) 'Infant and toddler mental health: models of clinical intervention with infants and their families', *Journal of Child Psychology and Psychiatry*, Vol. 44, No. 6, p. 926

Balbernie, R. (2008) 'Early intervention services: an overview of evidence-based practice', *Newsletter of the World Association for Infant Mental Health*, pp. 13–19

Bancroft, A. and Wilson, S. (2007) 'The "risk gradient" in policy on children of drug and alcohol users: framing young people as risky', *Health, Risk and Society*, Vol. 9, pp. 311–22

Bandura, A. (1977) *Social Learning Theory*, Englewood Cliffs, NJ: Prentice Hall

Barker, D. J., Eriksson, J. G., Forsen, T. and Osmond, C. (2002) 'Foetal origins of adult disease: strength of effects and biological basis', *International Journal of Epidemiology*, Vol. 31, pp. 1235–9

Barlow, J., Davis, H., McIntosh, E., Jarrett, P., Mockford, C. and Stewart-Brown, S. (2007) 'Role of home visiting in improving parenting and health in families at risk of abuse and neglect: results of a multicentre randomised controlled trial and economic evaluation', *Archives of Disease in Childhood*, Vol. 92, pp. 229–33

Barlow, J., Johnston, I., Kendrick, D., Polnay, L. and Stewart-Brown, S. (2008)

'Individual and group-based parenting programmes for the treatment of physical child abuse and neglect', Cochrane Database of Systematic Reviews, Issue 4

Barlow, J. and Schrader-MacMillan, A. (2009) *Safeguarding Children from Emotional Abuse – What Works?*, London: Department for Children, Schools and Families

Barlow, J., Simkiss, D. and Stewart-Brown, S. (2006) 'Interventions to prevent or ameliorate child physical abuse and neglect: findings from a systematic review of reviews', *Journal Children's Services*, Vol. 1, pp. 6–28

Barnard, M. and McKeganey. N. (2002) 'The impact of parental problem drug use on children: what is the problem and what can be done to help?', *Addiction*, Vol. 99, pp. 552–9

Barr, R. G., Rivara, F. P. and Barr, M. (2009) 'Effectiveness of educational materials designed to change knowledge and behaviours regarding crying and shaken-baby syndrome in mothers of newborns: a randomized, controlled trial', *Paediatrics*, Vol. 123, pp. 972–80

Barter, C. and McCarry, M. (2012) 'Love, power and control: experiences of partner violence and control', in Lombard, N. (2012) *Violence Against Women: Current Theory and Practice in Domestic Abuse, Sexual Violence and Exploitation, Research Highlights in Social Work*, London: Jessica Kingsley

Barter, C., McCarry, M., Berridge, D. and Evans, K. (2009) *Partner Exploitation and Violence in Teenage Intimate Relationships*, London: NSPCC

Bass, C. and Glaser, D. (2014) 'Early recognition and management of fabricated or induced illness in children', *The Lancet*, Vol. 383, pp. 1412–21

Bass, C. and Jones, D. (2011) 'Psychopathology of perpetrators of fabricated or induced illness in children: Case series', *British Journal of Psychiatry*, Vol. 199, pp. 113–18; doi: 10.1192/bjp. bp.109.074088

Beaulaurier, R. L., Seff, L. R., Newman, F. L. and Dunlop, B. D. (2007) 'External barriers to help seeking for older women who experience intimate partner violence', *Journal of Family Violence*, Vol. 22, pp. 747–55

Beddoe, L., Davys, A. and Adamson, C. (2011) 'Educating emotionally resilient practitioners', *Social Work Education*, Vol. 32, No. 1, pp. 100–17

Belsky, J., Houts, R. M. and Fearon, R. M. P. (2010) 'Infant attachment security and the timing of puberty: testing an evolutionary hypothesis', *Psychological Science*, Vol. 21, pp. 1195–1202

Benard, B. (2006) 'Using strengths-based practice to tap the resilience of families', in Saleebey, D. (ed.) (2006) *Strengths Perspective in Social Work Practice*, Boston, MA: Allyn and Bacon, pp. 197–220

Benger, J. and Pearse, A. (2002) 'Quality improvement report: simple intervention to improve detection of child abuse in emergency departments', *BMJ*, Vol. 324, pp. 780–2

Berrington, A., Diamond, I., Ingham, R., Stevenson, J., Borgoni, R., Cobos Hernández, M. I. and Smith, P. W. F. (2005) *Consequences of Teenage Parenthood: Pathways Which Minimise the Long Term Negative Impacts of Teenage Childbearing*, London: Department of Health

Bilukha, O., Hahn, R. A., Crosby, A., Fullilove, M. T., Liberman, A., Moscicki, E., Snyder, S., Tuma, F., Corso, P., Schofield, A. and Briss, P. A. (2005) 'The effectiveness of early childhood home visitation in preventing violence: A systematic review', *American Journal of Preventive Medicine*, Vol. 28, pp. 11–39

Biron, D. and Skelton, D. (2005) 'Perpetrator accounts in infant abusive head trauma brought about by a shaking event', *Child Abuse & Neglect*, Vol. 29, pp. 1347–58

Black, D. A., Smith Slep, A. M. and Heyman, R. E. (2001) 'Risk factors for child psychological abuse', *Aggression and Violent Behaviour*, Vol. 6, pp. 121–88

Bonomi, A., Anderson, M., Rivara, F. *et al.* (2008a) 'Health care utilization and costs associated with childhood abuse', *Journal of General Internal Medicine*, Vol. 23, pp. 294–9

Bonomi, A, Cannon, E., Anderson, M. *et al.* (2008b) 'Association between self-reported health and physical and/or sexual abuse experienced before age 18', *Child Abuse & Neglect*, Vol. 32, pp. 693–701

Bowlby, J. (1969) *Attachment*, New York, NY: Basic Books

Bowlby, J. (1978) 'Attachment theory and its therapeutic implications', in Feinstein, S. C. and Giovacchini, P. L. (eds) (1978) *Adolescent Psychiatry: Development and Clinical Studies*, Chicago, IL: University of Chicago Press

Bowlby, J. (1979) *The Making and Breaking of Affectional Bonds*, London: Tavistock

Bowlby, J. (1988) *A Secure Base: Parent-Child Attachment and Healthy Human Development*, New York, NY: Basic Books

Bowlby, R. and King, P. (2004) *Fifty Years of Attachment Theory: Recollections of Donald Winnicott and John Bowlby*, London: Allen Press

Brandon, M., Bailey, S. and Belderson, P. (2009) *Building on the Learning From Serious Case Reviews: A Two Year Analysis of Child Protection Database Notifications 2007–2009*, London: Department for Education

Brandon, M., Sidebotham, P., Ellis, C., Bailey, S. and Belderson, P. (2011) *Child and Family Practitioners' Understanding of Child Development: Lessons Learnt from a Small Sample of Serious Case Reviews*, London: Department for Education

Brandon, M. and Thoburn, J. (2008) 'Safeguarding children in the UK: a longitudinal study of services to children suffering or likely to suffer significant harm', *Child Family Social Work*, Vol. 13, pp. 365–77

Breslau, N. and Davis, G. C. (1987) 'Posttraumatic stress disorder: the etiologic specificity of wartime stressors', *American Journal of Psychiatry*, Vol. 144, pp. 578–88

Briere, J. (1996) *Trauma Symptoms Checklist for Children (TSCC) Professional Manual, Psychological Assessment Resources*, Lutz, FL: Odessa

British Medical Association (1998) *Domestic Violence: A Healthcare Issue?*, London: British Medical Association

Britner, P. A. and Reppucci, N. D. (1997) 'Prevention of child maltreatment: Evaluation of a parent education program for teen mothers', *Journal of Child and Family Studies*, Vol. 6, pp. 165–76

Brodsky, B. S. and Stanley, B. (2008) 'Adverse childhood experiences and suicidal behaviour', *Psychiatric Clinics of North America*, Vol. 31, pp. 223–35

Bronfenbrenner, U. (1979) *The Ecology of Human Development: Experiments by Nature and Design*, Cambridge, MA: Harvard University Press

Bronfenbrenner, U. (1986) 'Ecology of the family as a context for human development: research perspectives', *Developmental Psychology*, Vol. 22, pp. 723–42

Bronfenbrenner, U. and Morris, P. A. (1998) 'The ecology of developmental processes', in Damon, W. and Learner, R. M. (eds) (1998) *Handbook of Child Psychology: Theoretical Models of Human Development*, New York, NY: Wiley, pp. 993–1028

Brooker, S., Cawson, P., Kelly, G. and Wattam, C. (2001) 'The prevalence of child abuse and neglect: a survey of young people', *International Journal of Market Research*, Vol. 43, pp. 249–89

Browne, K., Hamilton-Giachritis, C. and Vettor, S. (2007) *Preventing Child Maltreatment in Europe: A Public Health Approach*, Copenhagen: World Health Organization

Bruffaerts, R., Demyttenaere, K., Borges, G., Haro, J. M., Chiu, W. T., Hwang, I., Karam, E. G., Kessler, R. C., Sampson, N., Alonso, J., Andrade, L. H., Angermeyer, M., Benjet, C., Bromet, E., de Girolamo, G., de Graaf, R., Florescu, S., Gureje, O., Horiguchi, I., Hu, C., Kovess, V., Levinson, D., Posada-Villa, J., Sagar, R., Scott, K., Tsang, A., Vassilev, S. M., Williams, D. R. and Nock, M. K. (2010) 'Childhood adversities as risk factors for onset and persistence of suicidal behaviour', *British Journal of Psychiatry*, Vol. 197, pp. 20–7; doi:10.1192/bjp.bp.109.074716

Buckley, H., Holt, S. and Whelan, S. (2007) 'Listen to me! Children's experiences of domestic violence', *Child Abuse Review*, Vol. 16, pp. 296–310

Bunting, L. (2011) *Sexual and Physical Violence against Children in Northern Ireland: A Statistical Overview of Recorded Crime 2008–10*, Belfast: NSPCC

Burghes, L. and Brown, M. (1995) *Single Lone Mothers: Problems, Prospects, and Policies*, London: Family Policy Studies Centre

Butchart, A. (2008) 'Epidemiology: the major missing element in the global response to child maltreatment?', *American Journal of Preventative Medicine*, Vol. 34, S103–S105

Butchart, A., Garcia-Moreno, C. and Mikton, C. (2010) *Preventing Intimate Partner and Sexual Violence Against Women*, Geneva: World Health Organization

Butchart, A., Harvey, A. P. and Fumiss, T. (2006) *Preventing Child Maltreatment: A Guide to Taking Action and Generating Evidence*, Geneva: World Health Organization and ISPCAN

Butchart, A. and Villaveces, A. (2003) *Violence against Women and the Risk of Infant and Child Mortality*, Geneva: World Health Organization

Caffy, J. (1946) 'Multiple fractures in the long bones of infants suffering from chronic subdural hematoma', *American Journal of Roentgen Radiological Therapy*, Vol. 56, pp. 163–73

Carpenter, G. L. and Stacks, A. M. (2009) 'Developmental effects of exposure to intimate partner violence in early childhood: a review of the literature', *Children and Youth Services Review*, Vol. 31, pp. 831–9

Carr, A, (2009) 'The effectiveness of family therapy and systemic interventions for adult-focused problems', *Journal of Family Therapy*, Vol. 31, pp. 46–74

Carter, J. and Schechter, S. (1997) *Child Abuse and Domestic Violence: Creating Community Partnerships for Safe Families-Suggested Components of an*

Effective Child Welfare Response to Domestic Violence, San Francisco, CA: Family Violence Prevention Fund

Cavanagh, K., Dobash, R. E. and Dobash, R. P. (2007) 'The murder of children by fathers in the context of child abuse', *Child Abuse & Neglect*, Vol. 31, pp. 731–46

Cawson, P., Wattam, C., Brooker, S. and Kelly, G. (2000) *Child Maltreatment in the United Kingdom: A Study of the Prevalence of Child Abuse and Neglect*, London: NSPCC

Cedeno, L. A., Elias, M. J., Kelly, S. and Chu, B. C. (2010) 'School violence, adjustment, and the influence of hope on low income, African American youth', *American Journal of Orthopsychiatry*, Vol. 80, pp. 213–26

CEMACH (2004) *Why Mothers Die 2000–2002*. Available from URL: www.hqip. org.uk/assets/NCAPOP-Library/CMACE-Reports/33.-2004-Why-Mothers-Die-2000–2002-The-Sixth-Report-of-the-Confidential-Enquiries-into-Maternal-Deaths-in-the-UK.pdf (accessed 25 July 2014)

Centre for Social Justice (2011) *Making Sense of Early Intervention*, London: CSJ

Chester, D. L., José, R, M., Aldlyami, E., King, H. and Moiemen, N. S. (2006) 'Non-accidental burns in children – Are we neglecting neglect?', *Burns*, Vol. 32, pp. 222–8

Christian, C., Block, R. and Committee on Child Abuse and Neglect (2009) 'Abusive head trauma in infants and children', *Paediatrics*, Vol. 123, pp. 1409–11

Cicchetti, D. (2013) 'Annual research review: resilient functioning in maltreated children – past, present and future perspectives', *Journal of Child Psychology and Psychiatry*, Vol. 54, pp. 402–22

Cicchetti, D. (2014) 'Illustrative development psychopathology perspectives on precursors and pathways to personality disorder', *Journal of Personality Disorders*, Vol. 28, pp. 172–9

Cicchetti, D. and Manley, J. T. (1990) 'A personal perspective on conducting research with maltreating families: problems and solutions', in Brody, G. and Sigel, I. (eds) (2014) *Methods of Family Research: Families At Risk*, Hillsdale, NJ: Lawrence Erlbaum Associates

Cicchetti, D., Rogosch, F. A. and Toth, S. L. (2006) 'Fostering secure attachment in infants in maltreating families through preventative interventions', *Development and Psychopathology*, Vol. 18, No. 3, pp. 623–49

Cicchetti, D. and Toth, S. L. (2005) 'Child maltreatment', Annual *Review of Clinical Psychology*, Vol. 1, pp. 409–38

Cicchetti, D. and Valentino, K. (2006) 'An ecological transactional perspective on child maltreatment', in Cicchetti, D. and Cohen, D. J. (eds) (2006) *Development Psychopathology*, New York, NY: Wiley, 2nd edn, pp. 129–291

Cleaver, H., Nicholson, D. and Tarr, S. (2006) *What Works? The Response of Children Protection Practices and Procedures to Children Exposed to Domestic Violence of Drug and Alcohol Within Their Families*, London: Royal Holloway, University of London

Cleaver, H., Unell, I. and Aldgate, J. (2011) *Children's Needs – Parenting Capacity: Parental Mental Illness, Learning Disability, Substance Misuse and Domestic Violence*, London: The Stationery Office, 2nd edn

Clinton, H. R. (2012) *Remarks at the International Day of Zero Tolerance for Female Genital Mutilation*. Available from URL: www.state.gov/secretary/20092013clinton/rm/2012/02/184071.htm (accessed 21 July 2014)

Coker, A. L., Davis, K. E., Arias, I. *et al.* (2002) 'Physical and mental health effects of intimate partner violence for men and women', *American Journal of Preventative Medicine*, Vol. 23, pp. 260–8

Collins, S. (2008) 'Social workers, resilience, positive emotions and optimism', *Practice: Social Work in Action*, Vol. 19, pp. 255–69

Collishaw, S., Pickles, A., Messer, J., Rutter, M., Shearer, C. and Maughan, B. (2007) 'Resilience to adult psychopathology following childhood maltreatment: evidence from a community sample', *Child Abuse & Neglect*, Vol. 31, pp. 211–29

Connell-Carrick, K. (2003) 'A critical review of the empirical literature: identifying correlates of child neglect', *Child and Adolescent Social Work Journal*, Vol. 20, pp. 389–425

Connelly, C. D. and Straus, M. A. (1992) 'Mothers age and risk for physical abuse', *Child Abuse & Neglect*, Vol. 16, pp. 709–18

Conrod, P. J., O'Leary-Barrett, M., Newton, N., Topper, L. M., Castellanos-Ryan, N., Mackie, C. and Girard, A. (2013) 'Effectiveness of a selective, personality-targeted prevention program for adolescent alcohol use and misuse: a cluster randomized controlled trial', *JAMA Psychiatry*, Vol. 70, pp. 334–42

Coohey, C. and Braun, N. (1997) 'Toward an integrated framework for understanding child physical abuse', *Child Abuse & Neglect*, Vol. 21, pp. 1081–94

Copello, A. G., Templeton, L. and Velleman, R. (2006) 'Family interventions for drug and alcohol misuse: is there a best practice?', *Current Opinion in Psychiatry*, Vol. 19, pp. 271–6

Corcoran, J. (2000) 'Family interventions with child physical abuse and neglect: a critical review', *Children and Youth Services Review*, Vol. 22, pp. 563–91

Coulton, C. J., Korbin, J. E., Su, M. and Chow, J. (1995) 'Community level factors and child maltreatment rates', *Child Development*, Vol. 66, pp. 1262–76

Creighton, S. (2004) *Prevalence and Incidence of Child Abuse: International Comparisons*, London: NSPCC

Crenshaw, W., Crenshaw, L. and Lichtenberg, J. (1995) 'When educators confront child abuse: an analysis of the decision to report', *Child Abuse & Neglect*, Vol. 19, p. 10

Crittenden, P. (1998) *Child Neglect: Causes and Contributions*, Thousand Oaks, CA: Sage

Crnic, K. A. and Greenberg, M. T. (1990) 'Minor parenting stresses with young children', *Child Development*, Vol. 61, pp. 1628–37

Crouch, J., Skowronski, J., Milner, J. and Harris, B. (2008) 'Parental responses to infant crying: the influence of child physical abuse risk and hostile priming', *Child Abuse & Neglect*, Vol. 32, pp. 702–10

Curenton, S. M., McWey, L. M. and Bolen, M. G. (2009) 'Distinguishing maltreating versus nonmaltreating at-risk families: implications for foster care and early childhood education interventions', *Families in Society*, Vol. 90, pp. 176–82

Cyr, C., Euser, E. M., Bakermans-Kranenburg, M. J. and Van Ijzendoorn, M.

H. (2010) 'Attachment security and disorganization in maltreating and high risk families: a series of meta-analyses', *Developmental Psychopathology*, Vol. 22 (Winter), pp. 87–108

Daniel, B. and Taylor, J. (2001) *Engaging with Fathers: Practice Issues for Health and Social Care*, London: Jessica Kingsley

Daniel, B., Taylor, J. and Scott, J. (2009) *Noticing and Responding to the Neglected Child*, London: Department for Children, Schools and Families and Department of Health

Daniel, B. and Wassell, S. (2002a) *The Early Years. Assessing and Promoting Resilience in Vulnerable Children 1*, London: Jessica Kingsley

Daniel, B. and Wassell, S. (2002b) *The School Years. Assessing and Promoting Resilience in Vulnerable Children 2*, London: Jessica Kingsley

Daniel, B. and Wassell, S. (2002c) *Adolescence. Assessing and Promoting Resilience in Vulnerable Children 3*, London: Jessica Kingsley

David, T. (2001) 'Shaken baby syndrome', in Gordon, R. and Harran, E. (eds) (2001) *Fragile Handle With Care*, London: NSPCC

De Bellis, M. D. (2001) 'Developmental traumatology: the psychobiological development of maltreated children and its implications for research, treatment and policy', *Development and Psychopathology*, Vol. 13, pp. 539–64

De Bellis, M. D. (2005) 'The psychobiology of neglect', *Child Maltreatment*, Vol. 10, pp. 150–72

De Bellis, M. D. and Thomas, L. (2003) 'Biologic findings of post-traumatic stress disorder and child maltreatment', *Current Psychiatry Reports*, Vol. 5, pp. 108–17

DePanfilis, D. and Dubowitz, H. (2005) 'Family connections: A programme for preventing child neglect', *Child Maltreatment*, Vol. 10, pp. 108–23

Department of Education (2010) *Building on the Learning from Serious Case Reviews: A Two Year Analysis of Child Protection Database Notifications 2007–2009*, London: Department for Education

Department of Health (2010) *Working Together to Safeguard Children. A Guide to Inter-Agency Working to Safeguard and Promote the Welfare of Children*, London: DH

Department of Health (2014) *Making Mental Health Services More Effective and Accessible*, London: DH

Department of Health Social Services and Public Safety (2009) *Families Matter: Supporting Families in Northern Ireland*, Belfast: DHSSPS

Devaney, J. (2009) 'Chronic child abuse and domestic violence: the characteristics and careers of children caught in the child protection system', *British Journal of Social Work*, Vol. 39, pp. 24–45

Devaney, J., Lazenbatt, A. and Bunting, L. (2011) 'Inquiring into non-accidental child deaths: reviewing the review process', *British Journal of Social Work*, Vol. 41, pp. 242–60

Devaney, J., Lazenbatt, A., Bunting, L., Davidson, G., Hayes, D. and Spratt, T. (in press) 'The relationship between cumulative adversity in childhood and adolescent suicide and accidental death', *Developing Practice*

Dias, M. S., Smith, K., DeGuehery, K. *et al.* (2005) 'Preventing abusive head trauma among infants and young children: a hospital-based parent education program', *Pediatrics*, Vol. 115, pp. 470–7

Dixon, L., Browne, K. and Hamilton-Giachritis, C. (2005) 'Risk factors of parents abused as children: a mediational analysis of the intergenerational continuity of child maltreatment (Part I)', *Journal of Child Psychology and Psychiatry*, Vol. 46, pp. 47–57

Dobash, R. and Dobash, R. (1992) *Women, Violence and Social Change*, London: Routledge

Dong, M., Anda, R. F., Felitti, V. J., Dube, S. R., Williamson, D. F. and Thompson, T. (2004) 'The inter-relatedness of multiple forms of childhood abuse, neglect and household dysfunction', *Child Abuse & Neglect*, Vol. 28, pp. 771–84

Dorkenoo, E. (2007) *A Statistical Study to Estimate the Prevalence of Female Genital Mutilation in England and Wales*, London: Forward

Dozier, M., Peloso, E. and Lewis, E. (2008) 'Effects of an attachment-based intervention on the cortisol production of infants and toddlers in foster care', *Development and Psychopathology*, Vol. 20 (Summer), pp. 845–59

Dozier, M., Peloso, E. and Lindhiem, O. (2006) 'Developing evidence-based interventions for foster children: An example of a randomized clinical trial with infants and toddlers', *Journal of Social Issues*, Vol. 62, pp. 767–85

Drake, B. and Pandey, S. (1996) 'Understanding the relationship between neighbourhood poverty and specific types of child maltreatment', *Child Abuse & Neglect*, Vol. 20, pp. 1003–18

Dube, S. R., Anda, R. F., Felitti, V. J., Croft, J. B., Edwards, V. J. and Giles, W. H. (2001) 'Growing up with parental alcohol abuse: Exposure to childhood abuse, neglect and household dysfunction', *Child Abuse & Neglect*, Vol. 25, pp. 1627–40

Dubowitz, H. (1990) 'Costs and effectiveness of interventions in child maltreatment', *Child Abuse & Neglect*, Vol. 14, pp. 177–86

Dubowitz, H., Lane, W., Semiatin, J. *et al.* (2011) 'The safe environment for every kid model: Impact of pediatric primary care professionals', *Pediatrics*, Vol. 127, No. 4, pp. e962–70

Duhaime, A. C., Gennarelli, T. A., Thibault, L. E., Marguiles, S. S. and Wiser, R. (1987) 'The shaken baby syndrome. a clinical, pathological and biomechanical study', *Journal of Neurosurgery*, Vol. 66, pp. 409–15

Duncan, R. D., Saunders, B. E., Kilpatrick, D. G., Hanson, R. F. and Resnick, H. S. (1996) 'Childhood physical assault as a risk factor for PTSD, depression, and substance abuse: findings from a national survey', *American Journal of Orthopsychiatry*, Vol. 66, pp. 437–48

Durlak, J. A. (1998) 'Common risk and protective factors in successful prevention programmes', *American Journal of Orthopsychiatry*, Vol. 68, pp. 512–20

Dutton, M. A. (1992) *Empowering and Healing the Battered Woman: A Model for Assessment and Intervention*, New York, NY: Springer

Edgeworth, J. and Carr, A. (2000) 'Child abuse', in Carr, A. (ed.) (2000) *What Works with Children and Adolescents? A Critical Review of Psychological Interventions with Children, Adolescents and their Families*, London: Routledge, pp. 17–48

Edleson, J. L. (1999) 'Children's witnessing of adult domestic violence', *Journal of Interpersonal Violence*, Vol. 14, pp. 839–87

Edleson, J. L. (2001) 'Studying the co-occurence of child maltreatment and women battering in families', in Graham-Bermann, S. A. and Edleson, J. L. (eds) (2001) *Domestic Violence in the Lives of Children: The Future of Research, Intervention and Social Policy*, Washington, DC: American Psychological Association, pp. 99–110

Edwards, V. J., Holden, G. W. and Felitti, V. J. (2003) 'Relationship between multiple forms of childhood maltreatment and adult mental health in community respondents: results from the adverse childhood experiences study', *American Journal of Psychiatry*, Vol. 160, pp. 1453–60

Elias, M. J., Zins, J. E., Weissberg, R. P., Frey, K. S., Greenberg, M. T., Haynes, N. M., Kessler, R., Schwab-Stone, M. E. and Shriver, T. P. (1997) *Promoting Social and Emotional Learning*, Alexandria, VA: Association for Supervision and Curriculum Development

Ellsberg, M., Jansen, H. A., Heise, L., Watts, C. H. and Garcia-Moreno, C. (2008) 'WHO Multi-country study on women's health and domestic violence against women study team: intimate partner violence and women's physical and mental health in the WHO multi-country study on women's health and domestic violence: An observational study', *The Lancet*, Vol. 371, pp. 1165–72

Evans, E., Hawton, K., Rodham, K. and Deeks, J. (2005) 'The prevalence of suicidal phenomena in adolescents: A systematic review of population-based studies', *Suicide and Life-Threatening Behaviour*, Vol. 35, No. 3, pp. 239–49

Farrell, A. D., Henry, D. B., Schoeny, M. E., Bettencourt, A. and Tolan, P. H. (2010) 'Normative beliefs and self-efficacy for nonviolence as moderators of peer, school, and parental risk factors for aggression in early adolescence', *Journal of Clinical Child and Adolescent Psychology*, Vol. 39, pp. 800–13

Feder, G., Ramsay, J., Dunne, D., Rose, M., Arsene, C. and Norman, R. (2009) 'How far does screening women for domestic (partner) violence in different health-care settings meet criteria for a screening programme? Systematic reviews of nine UK national screening committee criteria', *Health Technology Assessment*, Vol. 13, pp. 137–347

Feldman, M. (2004) *Playing Sick?: Untangling the Web of Munchausen Syndrome, Munchausen by Proxy, Malingering, and Factitious Disorder*, New York, NY: Brunner-Routledge

Feldman, M., Rosenquist, P. and Bond, J. (2001) 'Concurrent factitious disorder and factitious disorder by proxy. Double jeopardy', *General Hospital Psychiatry*, Vol. 19, pp. 24–8

Feldman-Jacobs, C. and Clifton, D. (2014) *Female Genital Mutilation/Cutting: Data and Trends Update 2014*, Washington, DC: Population Reference Bureau

Felitti, V. J. (2002) 'The relationship of adverse childhood experiences to adult health: turning gold into lead', *Zeitschrift für Psychosomatische Medizin und Psychotherapie*, Vol. 48, pp. 359–69

Felitti, V. J., Anda, R. F. and Nordenberg, D. (1998) 'Relationship of childhood abuse and household dysfunction to many of the leading causes of death in adults: the adverse childhood experiences (ACE) study', *American Journal of Preventative Medicine*, Vol. 14, pp. 245–58

Fergus, S. and Zimmerman, M. (2005) 'Adolescent resilience: a framework for understanding healthy development in the face of risk', *Annual Review of Public Health*, Vol. 26, pp. 399–419

Fergusson, D. M., Boden, J., Howwood, L. J. (2012) *Early Start Evaluation Report. Nibe Year Follow-Up, Christchurch Health and Development Study*, Dunedin: University of Otago

Fergusson, D. M. and Horwood, L. J. (1998) 'Exposure to interparental violence in childhood and psychosocial adjustment in young adulthood', *Child Abuse & Neglect*, Vol. 22, pp. 339–57

Fink, A. and McCloskey, L. (1990) 'Moving child abuse and neglect prevention programs forward: improving program evaluations', *Child Abuse & Neglect*, Vol. 14, pp. 187–206

Finkelhor, D. (1991) 'Child sexual abuse', in Rosenberg, M. and Fenley, M. A. (eds) (1991) *Violence in America. A Public Health Approach*, New York, NY: Oxford University Press, pp. 79–94

Finkelhor, D. (2008) *Childhood Victimisation*, Oxford: Oxford University Press

Finkelhor, D. and Ormrod, R. (2010) 'Poly-victimization in a national sample of children and youth', *American Journal of Preventive Medicine*, Vol. 38, pp. 323–30

Finkelhor, D, Turner, H. A., Shattuck, A. and Hamby, S. L. (2013) 'Violence, crime, and abuse exposure in a national sample of children and youth: an update', *JAMA Paediatrics*, Vol. 167, pp. 614–21

Flaherty, A. G., Sege, R. D,, Griffith, J., Price, L. L., Wasserman, R. and Wasserman, E. S. (2008) 'From suspicion of physical child abuse to reporting: primary care clinician decision-making', *Paediatrics*, Vol. 122, pp. 611–19

Flaherty, A. G., Sege, R. D. and Hurley, T. P. (2009) 'Translating child abuse research into action', *Paediatrics*, Vol. 122, S1–5

Flynn, S., Shaw, J. and Abel, K. (2013) 'Filicide: mental illness in those who kill their children', *PLOS ONE*, Vol. 8, p. e58981

Foerster, B., Petrou, M. and Lin, D. (2009) 'Neuroimaging evaluation of non-accidental head trauma with correlation to clinical outcomes: a review of 57 cases', *Journal of Paediatrics*, Vol. 154, pp. 573–7

Fonagy, P, Gergely, G., Jurist, E. L. and Target, M. (2002a) *Affect Regulation, Mentalization and the Development of the Self*, New York, NY: Other Press

Fonagy, P., Steele, M., Steele, H., Higgit, A. and Target, M. (1994) 'The theory and practice of resilience', *Journal of Child Psychology and Psychiatry*, Vol. 35, pp. 231–57

Fonagy, P., Target, M., Cottrell, D., Phillips, J. and Kurtz, Z. (2002b) *What Works For Whom? A Critical Review of Treatments for Children and Adolescents*, London: Guildford Press

Forrester, D. (2000) 'Parental substance misuse and child protection in a British sample. A survey of children on the Child Protection Register in an Inner London District Office', *Child Abuse Review*, Vol. 9, pp. 235–46

Forrester, D. (2007) 'Patterns of re-referral to social services: a study of 400 closed cases', *Child and Family Social Work*, Vol. 12, pp. 11–21

Forrester, D. and Williams, A. (2010) *Intensive Family Preservation Services and the 'Option 2' Model: A Practical Guide for IFS Teams*, London: University of Bedfordshire

FORWARD (2009) *FGM is Always with Us: Experiences, Perceptions and Beliefs of Women Affected by Female Genital Mutilation in London: Results from a PEER Study*, London: FORWARD

Francis, C., Hughes, H. and Hitz, L. (1992) 'Physically abusive parents and the 16-PF: a preliminary psychological typology', *Child Abuse & Neglect*, Vol. 16, pp. 673–91

Freisthler, B., Merritt, D. and LaScala, E. (2006) 'Understanding the ecology of child maltreatment: a review of the literature and directions for future research', *Child Maltreatment*, Vol. 11, pp. 263–80

Furstenberg, F. F., Brooks-Gunn, J. and Morgan, S. P. (1987) *Adolescent Mothers in Later Life*, Cambridge: Cambridge University Press

Galvani, S. (2004) 'Responsible disinhibition: Alcohol, men and violence to women', *Addiction Research and Theory*, Vol. 12, pp. 357–71

Galvani, S. (2010) *Supporting Families Affected by Substance Use and Domestic Violence*, Bedford: University of Bedfordshire

Garbarino, J. and Kostelny, K. (1992) 'Child maltreatment as a community problem', *Child Abuse & Neglect*, Vol. 16, pp. 455–64

Garmezy, N., Masten, A. S. and Tellegen, A. (1984) 'The study of stress and competence in children: a building block for developmental psychopathology', *Child Development*, Vol. 55, pp. 97–111

Garner, A. S., Shonkoff, J. P. *et al.* (2012) 'Early childhood adversity, toxic stress, and the role of the paediatrician: translating developmental science into lifelong health', *Paediatrics*, Vol. 129, e224–e231

Gask, L., Bower, P., Lamb, J., Burroughs, H., Chew-Graham, C., Edwards, S., Hibbert, D., Lovandzic, M., Lovell, K., Rogers, A., Waheed, W., Dowrick, C. and AMP Research Group (2012) 'Improving access to psychosocial interventions for common mental health problems in the United Kingdom: narrative review and development of a conceptual model for complex interventions', *BMC Health Services Research*, Vol. 12, pp. 249–62

Gazmararian, J. A. (2000) 'Violence and reproductive health; current knowledge and future research directions', *Maternal and Child Health Journal*, Vol. 4, pp. 79–84

Gazmararian, J. A., Lazorick, S. and Spitz, A. M. (1996) 'Prevalence of violence against pregnant women: a review of the literature', *Journal of the American Medical Association*, Vol. 275, pp. 1915–20

Geeraert, L., Van den Noortgate, W., Grietens, H. and Onghena, P. (2004) 'The effects of early prevention programs for families with young children at risk for physical child abuse and neglect: A meta-analysis', *Child Maltreatment*, Vol. 9, pp. 277–91

Ghate, D. (2000) 'Family violence and violence against children. Research review', *Children and Society*, Vol. 14, pp. 395–403

Ghate, D. and Hazel, N. (2002) *Parenting in Poor Environments: Stress, Support, and Coping*, London: Jessica Kingsley

Giardino, A. and Giardino, E. (2010) 'Child abuse and neglect, physical abuse', *eMedicine Pediatrics*, Vol. 915664, pp. 1–42

Gilbert, R., Kemp, A. and Thoburn, J. (2009) 'Recognizing and responding to child maltreatment', *The Lancet*, Vol. 373, pp. 167–80

Gladstone, B. M., Boydell, K. M. and McKeever, P. (2006) 'Recasting research into children's experiences of parental mental illness: Beyond risk and resilience', *Social Science and Medicine*, Vol. 62, pp. 2540–50

Glaser, D. (2000) 'Child abuse and neglect and the brain – a review', *Journal of Child Psychology and Psychiatry*, Vol. 41, pp. 97–116

Glaser, D. (2002) 'Emotional abuse and neglect (psychological maltreatment) a conceptual framework', *Child Abuse & Neglect*, Vol. 26, pp. 697–714

Glaser, D. (2007) 'The effects of child maltreatment on the brain', *The Link*, Vol. 16, pp. 1–4

Glowinski, A. L., Bucholz, K. K., Nelson, E. C., Fu, Q., Madden, P. and Reich, W. (2001) 'Suicide attempts in an adolescent female twin sample', *Journal of the American Academy of Child and Adolescent Psychiatry*, Vol. 40, pp. 1300–7

Golden, J. (2005) Message in a Bottle. The Making of Fetal Alcohol Syndrome, Cambridge, MA: Harvard University Press

Golding, K. (2004) 'Children experiencing adverse parenting early in life: the story of attachment', *Clinical Psychology*, Vol. 5, pp. 21–3

Goldstein, S. and Brooks, R. B. (2005) *Handbook of Resilience in Children*, New York, NY: Kluwer Academic/Plenum Publishers

Goodall, E. and Lumley, T. (2007) *'Not Seen and Not Heard' Child Abuse: A Guide for Donors and Funders*, London: New Philanthropies Capital

Gorin, S. (2004) *Understanding What Children Say: Children's Experiences of Domestic Violence, Parental Substance Misuse and Parental Health Problems*, York: National Children's Bureau, Joseph Rowntree Foundation

Grant, L. and Kinman, G. (2012) 'Enhancing wellbeing in social work students; building resilience in the next generation', *Social Work Education: The International Journal*, Vol. 31, p. 5; doi.org/10.1080/02615479.2011.590931

Gutman, L., Sameroff, A. and Eccles, J. (2002) 'The academic achievement of African-American students during early adolescence: an examination of multiple risk, promotive, and protective factors', *American Journal of Community Psychology*, Vol. 30, pp. 367–99

Haegerich, T. M. and Dahlberg, L. L. (2011) 'Violence as a public health risk', *American Journal of Lifestyle Medicine*, Vol. 5, pp. 392–406

Hardiker, P., Exton, K. and Barker, M. (1991) 'The social policy contexts of prevention in childcare', *British Journal of Social Work*, Vol. 21, pp. 341–59

Harlow, H. F. (1971) *Learning to Love*, San Francisco, CA: Albion

Harris, S. M. and Dersch, D. (2001) 'I'm just not like that': investigating the inter-generational cycle of violence', *The Family Journal*, Vol. 9, pp. 250–8

Hartley, C. C. (2002) 'The co-occurrence of child maltreatment and domestic violence: examining both neglect and child physical abuse', *Child Maltreatment*, Vol. 7, pp. 349–58

Hartley, C. C. (2004) 'Severe domestic violence and child maltreatment: considering child physical abuse, neglect, and failure to protect', *Children and Youth Services Review*, Vol. 23, pp. 373–92

Hazler, R. J. and Denham, S. A. (2002) 'Social isolation of youth at risk: conceptualizations and practical implications', *Journal of Counseling and Development*, Vol. 80, pp. 403–9

Hecht, D. B. and Hansen, D. J. (2001) 'The environment of child maltreatment:

contextual factors and the development of psychopathology', *Aggression and Violent Behaviour*, Vol. 6, pp. 433–57

Heckman, J. J. (2008) 'Role of income and family influence on child outcomes', *Annals of New York Academy of Science*, Vol. 1136, pp. 307–23

Heckman, J. J., Stixrud, J. and Urzua, S. (2006) 'The effects of cognitive and non-cognitive abilities on labour market outcomes and social behaviour', *Journal of Labor Economics*, Vol. 24, pp. 411–82

Heim, C. and Nemeroff, C. B. (2001) 'The role of childhood trauma in the neurobiology of mood and anxiety disorders: preclinical and clinical studies', *Biological Psychiatry*, Vol. 49, pp. 1023–39

Herman, H., Stewart, D., Diaz-Granados, N., Berger, N. and Jackson, Y. (2011) 'What is resilience?', *Canadian Journal of Psychiatry*, Vol. 56, pp. 258–65

Herrenkohl, E. C., Herrenkohl, R. C., Egolf, B. P. and Russo, M. J. (1998) 'The relationship between early maltreatment and teenage parenthood', *Journal of Adolescence*, Vol. 21, pp. 291–303

Hesse, E., and Main, M. (2006). 'Frightened, threatening, and dissociative parental behaviour in low-risk samples: description, discussion, and interpretations', *Development and Psychopathology*, Vol. 18, pp. 309–43

Hester, M., Pearson, C., Harwin, N. and Abrahams, H. (2006) *Making an Impact – Children and Domestic Violence*, 2nd edn, London: Jessica Kingsley

Hester, M., Pearson, C., Harwin, N., Doble, J., Fisher, U. and Hendry, E. (1998) *Making an Impact: Children and Domestic Violence*, Ilford: Barnardos/NSPCC

Hildan, Z., Smith, G., Netuveli, G. and Blane, D. (2008) 'Understanding adversity and resilience in older ages', *Sociology of Health and Illness*, Vol. 30, pp. 726–40

HM Government (2005) *The Adoption and Children Act 2002*, London: The Stationery Office

HM Government (2011) *Multi-Agency Practice Guideline: Female Genital Mutilation*, London: The Stationery Office

HMCPSI and HMIC (2004) *Violence at Home*, London: The Stationery Office

Holt, S., Buckley, H. and Whelan, S. (2008) 'The impact of exposure to domestic violence on children and young people: a review of the literature', *Child Abuse & Neglect*, Vol. 32, pp. 792–810

Home Office (2007) *Cross-Government Action Plan on Sexual Violence and Abuse*, London: The Stationery Office

Home Office (2010) *What is Domestic Violence?*, London: The Stationery Office

Home Office (2012) *Crime Survey for England and Wales 2010–11*, London: Home Office

Hooper, C.-A., Gorin, S., Cabral, C. and Dyson, C. (2007) *Living with Hardship 24/7: The Diverse Experiences of Families in Poverty in England*, London: Frank Buttle Trust

Hosking, G. and Walsh, I. (2005) *Tackling the Roots of Violence: Violence and What To Do About It: The WAVE Report*, Wave Trust: London

Howard, K. S. and Brooks-Gunn, J. (2009) 'The role of home-visiting programs in preventing child abuse and neglect', *The Future of Children*, Vol. 19, No. 2, p.119–46

Howard, L. M., Oram, S., Galley, H. and Feder, G. (2013) 'Domestic violence and perinatal mental disorders: a systematic review and meta-analysis', *PLOS Medicine*, Vol. 10

Howard, L. M., Trevillion, K. and Agnew-Davies, R. (2010) 'Domestic violence and mental health', *International Review Psychiatry*, Vol. 22, pp. 525–34

Humphreys, C. (2005) 'Relevant evidence for practice working with domestic violence and child abuse', in Humphreys, C. and Stanley, N. (eds) (2005) *Child Protection and Domestic Violence: Directions for Good Practice*, London: Jessica Kingsley

Humphreys, C., Houghton, C. and Ellis, J. (2008) *Literature Review: Better Outcomes for Children and Young People Experiencing Domestic Abuse*, Edinburgh: Scottish Executive Domestic Abuse Delivery Group, Scottish Government

Humphreys, C., Mullender, A. Houghton. C. and Ellis, J. (2002) 'Children's perspectives on domestic violence', in Humphreys, C., Houghton, C. and Ellis, J. (2008) *Literature Review: Better Outcomes for Children and Young People Experiencing Domestic Abuse – Directions for Good Practice*, Scotland: RR Donnelley

Humphreys, C., Thiara, R. K., Skamballis, A. and Mullender, A. (2006) *Talking about Domestic Abuse: A Photo Activity Workbook to Develop Communication Between Mothers and Young People*, London: Jessica Kingsley

Hunt, S. and Martin, A. (2001) *Pregnant Women, Violent Men: What Midwives Need to Know*, Hale: Books for Midwives

Jasinski, J. L. (2004) 'Pregnancy and domestic violence: a review of the literature', *Trauma Violence Abuse*, Vol. 5, pp. 47–64

Johnson, C. F. (2002) 'Child maltreatment 2002: recognition, reporting and risk', *Paediatrics International*, Vol. 44, pp. 554–60

Johnson, R., Rew, L. and Sternglanz, R. W. (2006) 'The relationship between childhood sexual abuse and sexual health practices of homeless adolescents', *Adolescence*, Vol. 41, pp. 221–34

Jonsson, E., Salmon, A. and Warren, K. (2014) 'The international charter on prevention of foetal alcohol spectrum disorder', *The Lancet*, Vol. 2, e135–e137

Jordan, B. and Sketchley, R. (2009) *A Stitch in Time Saves Nine: Preventing and Responding to the Abuse and Neglect of Infants*, NCPC Issues No. 30, Melbourne: National Child Protection Clearinghouse

Jütte, S., Bentley, H., Miller, P. and Jetha, N. (2013) *How Safe Are Our Children?*, London: NSPCC

Katz, I. (2007) *The Relationship Between Parenting and Poverty*, York: Joseph Rowntree Foundation. Available from URL: www.jrf.org.uk/bookshop/ebooks/parenting-poverty.pdf (accessed 18 June 2014)

Kaufman, J. and Zigler, E. (1987) 'Do abused children become abusive parents?', *American Journal of Orthopsychiatry*, Vol. 57, pp. 186–92

Kelley, B. T., Thornberry, T. P. and Smith, C. A. (1997) *In the Wake of Childhood Maltreatment*, Washington, DC: National Institute of Justice

Kemp, A., Dunstan, F., Harrison, S., Morris, S., Mann, M., Rolfe, K., Thomas, D. P., Sibert, J. and Maguire, S. (2008) 'Patterns of skeletal fractures in child abuse: systematic review', *BMJ*, Vol. 337, a1518

Kemp, A. M., Stoodley, N., Cobley. C., Coles, L. and Kemp, K. (2003) 'Apnoea and brain swelling in non-accidental head injury', *Archives of Disease in*

*Child*hood, Vol. 88, pp. 472–6

Kendall-Tackett, K. A. (2001) 'Physiological correlates of childhood abuse: chronic hyper-arousal in PTSD, depression, and irritable bowel syndrome', *Child Abuse & Neglect*, Vol. 24, pp. 799–810

Kendall-Tackett, K. A. (2002) 'The health effects of childhood abuse: four pathways by which abuse can influence health', *Child Abuse & Neglect*, Vol. 26, pp. 715–29

Kendall-Tackett, K. A. (2003) *Treating the Lifetime Health Effects of Childhood Victimization*, Kingston, NJ: Civic Research Institute Inc.

Kendler, K. S. and Gardner, C. O. (1998) 'Twin studies of adult psychiatric and substance dependence disorders: are they biased by differences in the environmental experiences of monozygotic and dizygotic twins in childhood and adolescence', *Psychological Medicine*, Vol. 28, pp. 625–33

Kendrick, D., Barlow, J., Hampshire, A., Polnay, L. and Stewart-Brown, S. (2007) 'Parenting interventions for the prevention of unintentional injuries in childhood', *Cochrane Database of Systematic Reviews*, Issue 4

Kennedy, I. (2010) *Getting It Right for Children and Young People: Overcoming Cultural Barriers in the NHS so as to Meet Their Needs*, London: Department of Health

Kinman, G. and Grant, L. (2011) 'Exploring stress resilience in trainee social workers: The role of social and emotional competencies', *British Journal of Social Work*, Vol. 41, No. 2, pp. 261–75

Kitzman, H., Olds, D. L., Henderson, C. R. Jr, Hanks, C., Cole, R., Tatelbaum, R., McConnochie, K. M., Sidora, K., Luckey, D. W., Shaver, D., Engelhardt, K., James, D. and Barnard, K. (1997) 'Effect of prenatal and infancy home visitation by nurses on pregnancy outcomes, childhood injuries, and repeated childbearing. A randomised controlled trial', *JAMA*, Vol. 278, pp. 644–52

Kitzman, K. M., Gaylord, N. K., Holt, A. R. and Kenny, E. D. (2003) 'Child witnesses to domestic violence: a meta-analytic review', *Journal of Consulting and Clinical Psychology*, Vol. 71, pp. 339–52

Klevens, J. and Whitaker, D. (2007) 'Primary prevention of child physical abuse and neglect: gaps and promising directions', *Child Maltreatment*, Vol. 12, pp. 364–77

Klohen, E. (1996) 'Conceptual analysis and measurement of the construct of ego resiliency', *Journal of Personality and Social Psychology*, Vol. 70, pp. 1067–79

Kotagal, U. R. (1993) 'Newborn consequences of teenage pregnancies', *Paediatric Annals*, Vol. 22, pp. 127–32

Kotch, J. B., Browne, D. C., Dufort, V., Winsor, J. and Catellier, D. (1999) 'Predicting child maltreatment in the first four years of life from characteristics assessed in the neonatal period', *Child Abuse & Neglect*, Vol. 23, pp. 305–19

Kroll, B. (2004) 'Living with an elephant: growing up with parental substance misuse', *Child and Family Social Work*, Vol. 9, pp. 129–40

Kroll, B. (2007) 'A family affair? Kinship care and parental substance misuse: some dilemmas explored', *Child and Family Social Work*, Vol. 12, pp. 84–93

Kroll, B. and Taylor, A. (2003) 'Parental substance misuse and child welfare', London: Jessica Kingsley

Krug, E. G., Mercy, J. A., Dahlberg, L. L. and Zwi, A. B. (2002) 'The world report on violence and health', *The Lancet*, Vol. 5, pp. 1083–8

Krugman, S. D., Lane, W. and Walsh, C. (2007) 'Update on child abuse prevention', *Current Opinion Paediatrics*, Vol. 19, pp. 711–18

Laing, L. (2000) 'Children, young people and domestic violence', *Issues Paper, No. 2*, Sydney: Australian Domestic and Family Violence Clearinghouse

Lasher, L. and Sheridan, M. (2004) *Munchausen by Proxy: Identification, Intervention and Case Management*, New York, NY: Haworth Maltreatment and Trauma Press

Layard, R., Clark, D., Knapp, M. and Mayraz, G. (2005) Cost–benefit analysis of psychological therapy, *National Institute Economic Review*, Vol. 202, pp. 90–8

Lazenbatt, A. (2010) 'What we know about the health and mental health effects of child sexual abuse on children', *Briefing Paper*, London: NSPCC

Lazenbatt, A. (2012) 'Impact of abuse and neglect on the health and well-being of children and young people', in Wilmer, G. (ed.) (2012) *Understanding and Treating the Lifelong Consequences of Childhood Sexual Abuse*, Leeds: The Lantern Project: Kilburn Prints

Lazenbatt, A., Bunting, L. and Taylor, J. (2012) 'Consequences of infant maltreatment on child well-being', *British Journal of Mental Health Nursing*, Vol. 1, pp. 171–5

Lazenbatt, A. and Freeman, R. (2006) 'Recognising and reporting child physical abuse: a survey of primary healthcare professionals', *Journal of Advanced Nursing*, Vol. 56, pp. 227–36

Lazenbatt, A. and Taylor, J. (2011) 'Fabricated induced illness in children', *Briefing Paper*, London: NSPCC

Lazenbatt, A. and Taylor, J. (2013) 'A critical review of fabricated induced illness in children', *Childcare in Practice*, Vol. 19, No. 1, pp. 61–77

Lazenbatt, A., Taylor, J. and Cree, L. (2009) 'A healthy settings framework: an evaluation and comparison of midwives' responses to addressing domestic violence', *Midwifery*, Vol. 25, pp. 622–36

Lea, A. (2011) *Families with Complex Needs: A Review of the Literature*, Leicester: Leicestershire County Council

Leeb, R. T., Lewis, T. and Zolotor, A. J. (2011) 'A review of physical and mental health consequences of child abuse and neglect and implications for practice', *American Journal of Lifestyle Medicine*, Vol. 5, pp. 454–61

Leverton, T. J. (2003) 'Parental psychiatric illness: the implications for children', *Current Opinion in Psychiatry*, Vol. 16, pp. 395–402

Lewis, G. and Drife, J. (2007) *Why Mothers Die 2000–2002? Report on Confidential Enquiries into Maternal Deaths in the United Kingdom*, London: CEMACH

Li, F., Godinet, M. T. and Arnsberger, P. (2011) 'Protective factors among families with children at risk of maltreatment: follow up to early school years', *Children and Youth Services Review*, Vol. 33, pp. 139–48

Lindberg, N., Laajasalo, T., Holi, M., Putkonen, H., Weizmann-Henelius, G. and Håkånen-Nyholm, H. (2009) 'Psychopathic traits and offended characteristics- a nationwide consecutive sample of homicidal male adolescents', *BMC Psychiatry*, Vol. 9, pp. 18–26

Litty, C. G., Kowalski, R. and Minor, S. (1996) 'Moderating effects of physical abuse and perceived social support on the potential to abuse', *Child Abuse & Neglect*, Vol. 20, pp. 305–14

Love, J. M., Kisker, E. E., Ross, C., Raikes, H., Constantine, J., Boller, K. *et al.* (2005) 'The effectiveness of early head start for 3-year-old children and their parents: Lessons for policy and programmes', *Developmental Psychology*, Vol. 41, pp. 885–901

Lubit, R., Rovine, D., DeFrancisci, L. and Eth, S. (2003) 'Impact of trauma on children', *Journal of Psychiatric Practice*, Vol. 9, pp. 128–38

Lundy, M. and Grossman, S. F. (2001) 'The mental health and service needs of young children exposed to domestic violence', *Families and Sociology*, Vol. 86, pp. 17–29

Luthar, S. S. (2006) 'Resilience in development: a synthesis of research across five decades', in Cicchetti, D. and Cohen, D. J. (eds) (2006) *Developmental Psychopathology: Risk, Disorder, and Adaptation*, New York, NY: Wiley, pp. 739–95

Luthar, S. S. and Zelazo, L. B. (2003) 'Research on resilience: an integrative review', in Luthar, S. S. (ed.) (2003) *Resilience and Vulnerability: Adaptation in the Context of Childhood Adversities*, Cambridge: Cambridge University Press, pp. 510–49

Lutzker, J. R. and Rice, J. M. (1984) 'Project 12-ways: measuring outcome of a large-scale in-home service for the treatment and prevention of child abuse and neglect', *Child Abuse & Neglect*, Vol. 8, pp. 519–24

MacIntyre, D. and Carr, A. (1999) 'Helping children to the other side of silence: a study of the impact of the stay safe programme on Irish children's disclosures of sexual victimization', *Child Abuse & Neglect*, Vol. 23, pp. 1327–40

MacLeod, J. and Nelson, G. (2000) 'Programs for the promotion of family wellness and the prevention of child maltreatment: a meta-analytical record', *Child Abuse & Neglect*, Vol. 24, pp. 1127–49

MacMillan, H., Fleming, J., Streiner, D., Lin, E., Boyle, M., Jamieson, E., Duku, E., Walsh, C., Wong, M. and Beardslee, W. (2001) 'Childhood abuse and lifetime psychopathology in a community sample', *American Journal of Psychiatry*, Vol. 158, pp. 1878–83

MacMillan, H. L., MacMillan, J. H., Offord, D. R., Griffith, L. and MacMillan, A. (1994) 'Primary prevention of child abuse and neglect: a critical review, part 1', *Journal of Child Psychology and Psychiatry and Allied Professions*, Vol. 35, pp. 835–76

MacMillan, H. L., Wathan, C. N., Barlow, J., Fergusson, D. M., Leventhal, J. M. and Taussig, H. N. (2009). Interventions to prevent child maltreatment and associated impairment. *Lancet*, 373, 250–266

MacMillan, R. (2009) 'The life course consequences of abuse, neglect, and victimization: Challenges for theory, data collection, and methodology', *Child Abuse & Neglect*, Vol. 32, pp. 661–5

Manlove, J. and Child Trends Incorporated (2002) *Preventing Teenage Pregnancy, Childbearing, and Sexually Transmitted Diseases: What the Research Shows*, Washington, DC: Child Trends Inc.

Manlove, J., Romano Papillo, A., Ikramullah, E. and National Campaign to

Prevent Teen Pregnancy (2004) *Not Yet: Programs to Delay First Sex Among Teens*, Washington, DC: National Campaign to Prevent Teen Pregnancy

Manning, V., Best, D. W., Faulkner, N. and Titherington, E. (2009) 'New estimates of the numbers of children living with substance misusing parents: results from UK national household surveys', *BMC Public Health*, Vol. 9

Marriott, C., Hamilton-Giachritsis, C. and Harrop, C. (2014) 'Factors promoting resilience following childhood sexual abuse: a structured, narrative review of the literature', *Child Abuse Review*, Vol. 23, pp. 17–34

Masten, A. S. (2007) 'Resilience in developing systems: progress and promise as the fourth wave rises', *Development and Psychopathology*, Vol. 19, pp. 921–39

Masten, A. S. (2012) 'Risk and resilience in development', in Zelazo, P. D. (ed.) (2012) *Handbook of Developmental Psychology*, Oxford: Oxford University Press

Masten, A. S. and Obradovic, J. (2006) 'Competence and resilience in development', *Annals of the New York Academy of Sciences*, Vol. 1094, pp. 13–27

Masten, A. S. and Wright, M. O. (1998) 'Cumulative risk and protection models of child maltreatment', *Journal of Aggression, Maltreatment and Trauma*, Vol. 2, pp. 7–30

Mauricio, A. M. and Gormley, B. (2001) 'Male perpetration of physical violence against female partners: the interaction of dominance needs and attachment insecurity', *Journal of Interpersonal Violence*, Vol. 16, pp. 1066–80

May-Chahal, C., Hicks, S. and Tomlinson, J. (2004) *The Relationship Between Child Death and Child Maltreatment. A Research Study on the Attribution and Cause of Death in Hospital Settings*, London: NSPCC

Mayer, J. D. and Salovey, M. (1997) 'What is emotional intelligence?', in Salovey, P. and Sluyter, D. (eds) (1997) *Emotional Development and Emotional Intelligence: Educational Implications*, New York, NY: Basic Books, pp. 3–31

McConnell, N., Taylor, J., Belton, E. and Barnard, M. (in press) 'Evaluating programmes for violent fathers: Challenges and ethical review', *Child Abuse Review*

McCosker-Howard, H. and Woods, A. (2006) 'How is intimate partner abuse experienced by childbearing women?', in Roberts, G., Hegarty, K. and Feder, G. (eds) (2006) *Intimate Partner Abuse and Health Professionals: New Approaches to Domestic Violence*, London: Churchill Livingstone

McDowell, J. and Lyons, F. (2009) 'Improving outcomes for young children: A review of evaluated interventions', in *Highlight, Belfast:* National Children's Bureau Northern Ireland, p. 247

McGee, C. (2000) *Childhood Experiences of Domestic Violence*, London: Jessica Kingsley

McGuigan, W. M. and Pratt, C. C. (2001) 'The predictive impact of domestic violence on three types of child maltreatment', *Child Abuse & Neglect*, Vol. 25, pp. 869–83

McIntosh, J. (2003) 'Children living with domestic violence: research foundations for early intervention', *Journal of Family Studies*, Vol. 9, 219–34

McManus, E., Belton, E., Barnard, M., Cotmore, R. and Taylor, J. (2013) 'Recovering from domestic abuse, strengthening the mother–child relationship: Mothers' and children's perspectives of a new intervention, Special issue:

Physical abuse in high risk families, *Child Care in Practice*, Vol. 19, No. 3, pp. 291–310

Melhuish, E., Belsky, J. and Leyland, A. (2008) *The Impact of Sure Start Local Programmes on Three Year Olds and their Families*, London: University of Birkbeck

Meltzer, H., Doos, L., Vostanis, P., Ford, T. and Goodman, R. (2009) 'The mental health of children who witness domestic violence', *Child and Family Social Work*, Vol. 4

Mersky, J. P., Berger, L. M., Reynolds, A. J. and Gromoske, A. N. (2009) 'Risk factors for child and adolescent maltreatment: A longitudinal investigation of a cohort of inner-city youth', *Child Maltreatment*, Vol. 14, pp. 73–88

Mezey, G. C., Bacchus, L. and Bewley, S. (2005) 'Domestic violence, lifetime trauma and psychological health of childbearing women', British Journal of Obstetrics and Gynaecology: An *International Journal of Obstetrics and Gynaecology*, Vol. 112, pp. 197–204

Mezey, G. C., Bacchus, L., Haworth, A. *et al.,* (2003) 'Midwives' perceptions and experiences of routine enquiry for domestic violence', *British Journal of Obstetrics and Gynaecology*, Vol. 110, pp. 744–52

Mezey, G. C. and Bewley, S. (1997) 'Domestic violence and pregnancy', *British Medical Journal*, Vol. 314, p. 1295

Mguni, N., Bacon, N. and Brown, J. F. (2012) *The Well-Being and Resilience Paradox*, London: Young Foundation

Mian, A. I. (2005) 'Depression in pregnancy and the postpartum period: balancing adverse effects of untreated illness with treatment risks', *Journal of Psychiatric Practice*, Vol. 11, pp. 389–96

Mikton, C. and Butchart, A. (2009) 'Child maltreatment prevention: a systematic review of reviews', *Bulletin of the World Health Organization*, Vol. 83, pp. 355–61

Milner, J. S. and Chilamkurti, C. (1991) 'Physical child abuse perpetrator characteristics: a review of the literature', *Journal of Interpersonal Violence*, Vol. 6, pp. 345–66

Milner, J. S. and Dopke, C. (1997) 'Child physical abuse: review of offender characteristics', in Wolfe, D. A., McMahon, R. J. and Peters, R. D. (eds) (1997) *Child Abuse: New Directions in Prevention and Treatment Across the Lifespan*, Thousand Oaks, CA: Sage, pp. 27–54

Milner, J. S., Robertson, K. R. and Rogers, D. L. (1990) 'Childhood history of abuse and adult child abuse potential', *Journal of Family Violence*, Vol. 5, pp. 15–34

Mirrlees-Black, C. (1999) *Domestic Violence: Findings from the British Crime Survey Self Completion Questionnaire*, London: Home Office

Montgomery, P., Gardner, F., Bjornstad, G. and Ramchandani, P. (2009) *Systematic Reviews of Interventions Following Physical Abuse: Helping Practitioners and Expert Witnesses Improve the Outcomes of Child Abuse*, London: Department for Children, Schools and Families

Moore, S. and Rosenthal, D. (1993) *Sexuality in Adolescence*, London: Routledge

Moran, P., Ghate, D. and van der Merwe, A. (2004) *What Works in Parenting Support? A Review of the International Evidence*, London: Policy Research

Bureau

Morris, K., Hughes, N., Clarke, H. *et al.* (2008) *Think Family: A Literature Review of Whole Family Approaches*, London: Cabinet Office

Mrazek, P. J. and Haggerty, R. J. (1994) *Reducing Risks for Mental Disorders: Frontiers for Preventative Intervention Research*, Washington DC: National Academy Press

Mullender, A. (2004) *Tackling Domestic Violence: Providing Support for Children Who Have Witnessed Domestic Violence*, London: Home Office

Mullender, A., Burton, S., Hague, G., Imam, U., Kelly, L., Malos, E. and Regan, L. (2003a) *Stop Hitting Mum!': Children Talk about Domestic Violence*, East Molesey, Surrey: Young Voice

Mullender, A., Hague, G., Iman, U., Kelly, L., Malos, E. and Regan, L. (2002) *Children's Perspectives on Domestic Violence*, Thousand Oaks, CA: Sage

Mullender, A., Hague, G., Imam, U., Kelly, L., Malos, E. and Regan, L. (2003b) 'Could have helped but they did not: the formal and informal support systems experienced by children living with domestic violence', in Hallett, C. and Prout, A. (eds) (2003) *Hearing the Voices of Children: Social Policy for a New Century*, London: Routledge Falmer

Munro, E., Taylor, J. and Bradbury-Jones, C. (2014) 'Understanding the causal pathways to child maltreatment', *Child Abuse Review*, DOI: 10.1002/car.2266

Murray, K. and Zautra, A. (2012) 'Community resilience: fostering recovery, sustainability, and growth', in Ungar, M. (ed.) (2012) *The Social Ecology of Resilience: A Handbook of Theory and Practice*, New York, NY: Springer, pp. 337–46

Murray, L. (2006) *Attachment and Mental Health: Background Paper for Conference on Early Development, Attachment and Social Policy*, Cambridge: University of Cambridge

Murray, L., Fiori-Cowley, A., Hooper, R. and Cooper, P. (1996) 'The impact of postnatal depression and associated adversity on early mother-infant interactions and later infant outcome', *Child Development*, Vol. 67, pp. 2512–26

National Commission of Inquiry into the Prevention of Child Abuse (1996) *Childhood Matters: The Report*, London: The Stationery Office

Neigh, G. N., Gillespie, C. F. and Nemeroff, C. B. (2009) 'The neurobiological toll of child abuse and neglect', *Trauma Violence Abuse*, Vol. 10, pp. 389–410

Nelson, C. and Bosquet, M. (2000) 'Neurobiology of foetal and infant development: implications for infant mental health', in Zeanah, C. (ed.) (2000) *Handbook of Infant Mental Health*, New York, NY: Guilford, pp. 37–59

NICE (2006) *Parent-Training/Education Programmes in the Management of Children with Conduct Disorders*, London: National Institute for Health and Clinical Excellence

NICE (2009) *When to Suspect Abuse – Clinical Guideline*, London: RGOG Press

Norman, R. E., Byambaa, M., De, R., Butchart, A., Scott, J. and Vos, T. (2012) 'The long-term health consequences of child physical abuse, emotional abuse, and neglect', *PLOS Medicine*, Vol. 9, e1001349

Oates, M. (2003) 'Suicide: the leading cause of maternal death', The *British Journal of Psychiatry*, Vol. 183, pp. 279–81

O'Connor, T. G., Davies, L., Dunn, J. and Golding, J. (2000) 'Distribution of accidents, injuries, and illnesses by family type', *Paediatrics*, Vol. 106

Office for National Statistics (2001) *Psychiatric Morbidity Survey*, London: ONS

Office for National Statistics (2014) *UK National Statistics*. Available from URL: www.statistics.gov.uk/hub/index.html (accessed 21 July 2014)

Ofsted (2010) *Learning Lessons from Serious Case Reviews: 2009–10*, London: Office for Standards in Education Children's Services and Skills

Ofsted (2011a) *Ages of Concern: Learning Lessons from Serious Case Reviews: A Thematic Report of Ofsted's Evaluation of Serious Case Reviews from 1 April 2007 to 31 March 2011*, London: Office for Standards in Education Children's Services and Skills

Ofsted (2011b) *The Voice of the Child: Learning Lessons from Serious Case Reviews*, London: Office for Standards in Education Children's Services and Skills

Olds, D. (1997) 'Long-term effects of home visitation on maternal life course and child abuse and neglect. Fifteen-year follow-up of a randomised trial', *JAMA*, Vol. 278, pp. 637–43

Olds, D. *et al.* (2002) 'Home visiting by paraprofessionals and by nurses: a randomised, controlled trial', *Pediatrics*, Vol. 110, pp. 486–96

Oliver, J. and Washington, K. T. (2009) 'Treating perpetrators of child physical abuse: A review of interventions', *Trauma, Violence & Abuse*, Vol. 10, pp. 115–24

Osofsky, J. D. (1993) 'Chronic community violence: What is happening to our children?', *Psychiatry*, Vol. 56, pp. 36–45

Osofsky, J. D. (2003) 'Prevalence of children's exposure to domestic violence and child maltreatment: implications for practice and intervention', *Clinical Child and Family Psychology Review*, Vol. 6, pp. 161–70

Osofsky, J. D., Hammer, J. H., Freeman, N. and Rovaris, J. M. (2004) 'How law enforcement and mental health professionals can partner to help traumatised children', in Osofsky, J. D. (ed.) (2004) *Young Children and Trauma: Intervention and Treatment*, New York, NY: Guilford Press, pp. 285–298

Osofsky, J. D. and Lieberman, A. F. (2011) 'A call for integrating a mental health perspective into systems of care for abused and neglected infants and young children', *American Psychologist* Vol. 66, pp. 120–8

Panter-Brick, C. and Leckman, J. (2013) 'Resilience in child development: Interconnected pathways to wellbeing, *Journal of Child Psychology and Psychiatry*, Vol. 54, No. 4, pp. 333–6

Parsons, S., Sullivan, A. and Brown, M. (2012) *Research on the British Cohort Study, 1970*. The Centre for Longitudinal Studies (CLS) is an Economic and Social Research Council (ESRC) Resource Centre based at the Institution of Education (IOE), University of London

Pence, E. and Paymer, M. (1993) *Education Groups for Men Who Batter: The Duluth Model*, New York, NY: Springer

Perroud, N., Courtet, P., Vincze, I., Jaussent, I., Jollant, F., Bellivier, F., Leboyer, M., Baud, P., Buresi, C. and Malafosse, A. (2007) 'Interaction between BDNF Val66Met and childhood trauma on adult's violent suicide attempt', *Genes, Brain and Behavior*, Vol. 7, pp. 314–22

Perry, B. (1996) *Maltreated Children: Experience, Brain Development and the*

Next Generation, New York, NY: Norton

Perry, B. (1998) *Biological Relativity: Time and the Developing Child*, Houston, TX: Civitas Child Trauma Programs

Perry, B. (2002) 'Childhood experience and the expression of genetic potential: what childhood neglect tells us about nature and nurture', *Brain and Mind*, Vol. 3, pp. 79–100

Perry, B. (2011) *Using a Neuro-Developmental Lens When Working With Children Who Have Experienced Maltreatment: A Review of the Literature*, Sydney, NSW: Research and Program Development Social Justice Unit

Perry, B., Pollard, R., Blakley, T. and Viglante, D. (1995) 'Childhood trauma, the neurobiology of adaptation, and "use-dependent" development of the brain: How "states" become "traits" ', *Infant Mental Health Journal*, Vol. 16, pp. 271–91

Perry, B. (2001) 'The neuro-developmental impact of violence in childhood', in Schetky, D. and Benedek, E. (eds) (2001) *Textbook of Child and Adolescent Forensic Psychia*try, Washington, DC: American Psychiatric Press, pp. 221–38

Perry, B. and Hambrick, E. P. (2008) 'The neurosequential model of therapeutics', *Youth for Change*, Vol. 17, p. 43

Phoenix, A. (1991) *Young Mothers*, Cambridge: Polity Press

Pico-Alfonso, M. A., Garcia-Linares, M. I., Celda-Navarro, N., Blasco-Ros, C., Echeburua, E. and Martinez, M. (2005) 'The impact of physical, psychological, and sexual intimate male partner violence on women's health: depressive symptoms, post-traumatic stress disorder, state anxiety, and suicide', *Journal of Women's Health*, Vol. 15, pp. 599–611

Police Service of Northern Ireland (2011) *Trends in Police Recorded Crime in Northern Ireland 1998/99 to 2010/11*, Belfast: Police Service of Northern Ireland

Pooley, L. and Cohen, L. (2010) 'Resilience: a definition in context', *Australian Community Psychologist*, Vol. 22, pp. 30–7

Porter, T. and Gavin, H. (2010) 'Infanticide and neonaticide: a review of 40 years of research literature on incidence and causes', *Trauma Violence and Abuse*, Vol. 11, pp. 99–112

Povey, E., Coleman, K., Kaiza, P., Hoare, C. and Jansson, K. (2008) *Home Office Statistical Bulletin: Crime in England and Wales 2006/07. Supplementary Volume 2 to Crime in England and Wales 2006/07*, London: The Stationery Office

Prange, M., Coats, B., Duhaime, A. and Marguiles, S. (2003) 'Anthropomorphic simulations of falls, shakes, and inflicted impacts in infants', *Journal of Neurosurgery*, Vol. 99, pp. 143–50

Pritchard, C. and Sharples, A. (2008) 'Violent deaths in England and Wales and the major developed countries 1974–2002: possible evidence of improving child protection?', *Child Abuse Review*, Vol. 17, pp. 297–312

Pritchard, C. and Williams, R. (2010) 'Comparing possible "child-abuse-related deaths" in England and Wales with the major developed countries 1974–2006: signs of progress?', *British Journal of Social Work*, Vol. 40, pp. 1700–18

Putnam-Hornstein E. P., Webster, D., Needell, B. and Magruder, J. (2011) 'A public health approach to child maltreatment surveillance: evidence from a data linkage project in the United States', *Child Abuse Review*, Vol. 20, pp. 231–306

Puttnam, R. (2000) *Bowling Alone – The Collapse and Revival of American Community*, New York, NY: Simon and Schuster

Radford L., Blacklock, N. and Iwi, K. (2006) 'Domestic abuse risk assessment and safety planning in child protection – assessing perpetrators', in Humphreys, C. and Stanley, N. (eds) (2006) *Domestic Violence and Child Protection: Directions for Good Practice*, London: Jessica Kingsley, pp. 171–89

Radford, L., Corral, S., Bredley, C., Fisher, H., Bassett, C. and Collishaw, S. (2011) *Child Abuse & Neglect in the UK Today*, London: NSPCC

Ransom, G., Mann, F. A., Vavilala, M. S., Haruff, R. and Rivara, F. P. (2003) 'Cerebral infarct in head injury: relationship to child abuse', *Child Abuse & Neglect*, Vol. 27, pp. 381–92

Read, J. (1998) 'Child abuse and the severity of disturbance among adult psychiatric inpatients', *Child Abuse & Neglect*, Vol. 22, pp. 359–68

Read, J., van Os, J., Morrison, A., and Ross, C. (2005) 'Childhood trauma, psychosis and schizophrenia: a literature review with theoretical and clinical implications', *Acta Psychiatrica Scandinavica*, Vol. 112, pp. 330–50

Redman, S. and Taylor, J. (2006) 'Legitimate family violence as represented in the print media: textual analysis', *Journal of Advanced Nursing*, Vol. 56, pp. 157–66

Resnick, M. D., Ireland, M. and Borowsky, I. (2004) 'Youth violence perpetration: what protects? What predicts? Findings from the national longitudinal study of adolescent health', *Journal of Adolescent Health*, Vol. 35, 424.e421

Resnick, P. J. (1970) 'Murder of the newborn: a psychiatric review of neonaticide', *American Journal of Psychiatry*, Vol. 126, pp. 1414–42

Reynolds, A. J., Mathieson, L. and Topitzes, J. (2009) 'Do early childhood interventions prevent child maltreatment? A review of research', *Child Maltreatment*, Vol. 14, No. 2, pp. 182–206

Reynolds, A. J. and Robertson, D. (2003) 'School-based early intervention and later child maltreatment in the Chicago longitudinal study', *Child Development*, Vol. 74, No. 1, pp. 3–26

Roehlkepartain, E. and Sesma, A. (2007) *Developmental Assets: A Framework for Enriching Service-Learning [online]*. Available from URL: www.servicelearning.org (accessed 1 August 2010)

Rogers, R. (2004) 'Diagnostic, explanatory, and detection models of Munchausen by proxy: extrapolations from malingering and deception', *Child Abuse & Neglect*, Vol. 28, pp. 225–30

Romito, P., Turan, J. M. and Marchi, M. D. (2005) 'The impact of current and past interpersonal violence on women's mental health', *Social Science and Medicine*, Vol. 60, pp. 1717–28

Rose, W. and Barnes, J. (2008) *Improving Safeguarding Practice: Study of Serious Case Reviews 2001–2003*, London: Department for Children Schools and Families

Rosenbaum, M. (1990) 'The role of depression in couples involved in murder-suicide and homicide', *American Journal of Psychiatry*, Vol. 147, pp. 1036–9

Rosenburg, D. (1987) 'Web of deceit: a literature review of Munchausen syndrome by proxy', *Child Abuse & Neglect*, Vol. 11, pp. 547–63

Royal College of Psychiatrists (2011a) *Anxiety, Panic, Phobias*, London: Royal College of Psychiatrists

Royal College of Psychiatrists (2011b) *Bipolar Disorder*, London: Royal College of Psychiatrists

Royal College of Psychiatrists (2011c) *Depression*, London: Royal College of Psychiatrists

Royal College of Psychiatry and Child Health (2004) *Responsibilities of Doctors in Child Protection Cases with Regard to Confidentiality*, London: Royal College of Paediatrics and Child Health

Runtz, M. G. and Schallow, J. R. (1997) 'Social support and coping strategies as mediators of adult adjustment following childhood maltreatment', *Child Abuse & Neglect*, Vol. 21, pp. 211–26

Russell, B. S., Britner, P. A. and Trudeau, J. J. (2008) 'Intervention type matters in primary prevention of abusive head injury: event history analysis results', *Child Abuse & Neglect*, Vol. 32, pp. 949–57

Rutter, M. (1979a) 'Maternal deprivation, 1972–1978: new findings, new concepts, new approaches', *Child Development*, Vol. 50, pp. 283–305

Rutter, M. (1979b) 'Protective factors in children's responses to stress and disadvantage', in Kent, M. W. and Rolf, J. E. (eds) (1979) *Primary Prevention of Psychopathology*, Hanover, NH: University of New England Press

Rutter, M. (1985) 'Resilience in the face of adversity: protective factors and resistance to psychiatric disorder', *British Journal of Psychiatry*, Vol. 147, pp. 598–611

Rutter, M. (2006) 'Implication of resilience concepts for scientific understanding', in Lester, B. M., Masten, A. S. and McEwan, B. (eds) (2006) *Resilience in Children*, Boston, MA: Blackwell

Rutter, M. (2007) 'Resilience, competence and coping', *Child Abuse & Neglect, Vol.* 31, pp. 205–9

Sabates, R. and Dex, S. (2012) *Multiple Risk Factors in Young Children's Development*, CLS Working Paper 2012/1, London: Centre for Longitudinal Studies

Sameroff, A., Bartko, W., Baldwin, A. *et al.* (1998) 'Family and social influence on the development of child competence', in Lewis, M. and Feiring, C. (eds) (1998) *Families, Risk, and Competence*, Hillsdale, NJ: Lawrence Erlbaum Associates, pp. 177–92

Sanders, G. (2006) *Twenty-Nine Child Homicides: Lessons Still To Be Learnt on Domestic Violence and Child Protection*, Bristol: Women's Aid Federation of England

Scannapieco, L. and Connell-Carrick, K. (2005) *Understanding child maltreatment. An ecological and developmental perspective*, New York, NY: Oxford University Press

Schore, A. N. (2001) 'The effects of early relational trauma on right brain development, affect regulation and infant mental health', *Infant Mental Health Journal*, Vol. 22, pp. 201–69

Schore, A. N. (2003) 'Early relational trauma, disorganized attachment, and the development of a predisposition to violence', in Solomon, M. F. and Siegel, D. J. (eds) (2003) *Healing Trauma: Attachment, Mind, Body, and Brain*, New

York, NY: Norton

Schore, A. N. (2009) *Affect Dysregulation and Disorders of the Self (Norton Series on Interpersonal Neurobiology)*. New York, NY: Norton

Schore, A. N. (2010) 'Synopsis', in Lanius, R. A., Vermetten, E. and Pain, C. (eds) (2010) *The Impact of Early Life Trauma on Health and Disease: The Hidden Epidemic*, Cambridge: Cambridge University Press

Schore, A. N. (2011) 'The right brain implicit self lies at the core of psychoanalysis', *Psychoanalytic Dialogues*, Vol. 21, pp. 75–100

Schore, A. N. and McIntosh, J. E. (2011) 'Family law and the neuroscience of attachment, part 1', *Family Court Review*, Vol. 49, pp. 501–12

Schreier, H. A. and Libow, J. A. (1993) *Hurting for Love: Munchausen by Proxy Syndrome*, New York, NY: Guilford Press

Scobie, R. and McGuire, M. (1999) 'The silent enemy: domestic violence in pregnancy', *British Journal of Midwifery*, Vol. 7, pp. 259–62

Scottish Government (2008) *Getting it Right for Every Child. Highland Pathfinder Guidance. Appendix 4. Using the Resilience Matrix.* Available from URL: www.forhighlandschildren.org/htm/girfec/gir-publications/GIRFEC%20 Guidance%20Mar%2008%20separate%20sections/girfec-hpguidance-app4. pdf (accessed 3 June 2009)

Scottish Government (2010) *Statistical Bulletin Crime and Justice Series: Homicide in Scotland, 2009–10*, Edinburgh: Scottish Government

Scottish Government (2013) *Getting Our Priorities Right: Updated Good Practice Guidance For All Agencies and Practitioners Working With Children, Young People and Families Affected by Problematic Alcohol and/or Drug Use*, Edinburgh: Scottish Government

Selph, S. S., Bougatsos, C., Blazina, I. and Nelson, H. D. (2013) 'Behavioural interventions and counselling to prevent child abuse and neglect: a systematic review to update the US preventative services task force recommendation', *Annals of Internal Medicine*, Vol. 158, pp. 179–90

Shadigian, E. M. and Bauer, S. T. (2004) 'Screening for partner violence during pregnancy', *International Journal of Gynaecology and Obstetrics*, Vol. 84, pp. 273–80

Shepherd, J. and Sampson, A. (2000) 'Don't shake the baby: towards a prevention strategy', *British Journal of Social Work*, Vol. 30, pp. 721–35

Sher, J. (2010) *Ten Facts about Foetal Alcohol Harm*, Edinburgh: Children in Scotland

Sheridan, M. (2002) 'The deceit continues: an updated literature review of Munchausen syndrome by proxy', *Child Abuse & Neglect*, Vol. 27, pp. 431–51

Shipman, K. L., Rossman, B. B. R. and West, J. C. (1999) 'Co-occurrence of spousal violence and child abuse: conceptual implications', *Child Maltreatment*, Vol. 4, pp. 93–102

Shonkoff, J. (2010) 'Building a new bio-developmental framework to guide the future of early childhood policy', *Child Development*, Vol. 81, pp. 357–67

Shonkoff, J. (2011) 'Protecting brains, not simply stimulating minds', *Science*, Vol. 333, pp. 982–3

Shonkoff, J., Garner, A. *et al.* (2012) 'The lifelong effects of early childhood adversity and toxic stress', *Pediatrics*, Vol. 129, No. 1, pp. e232–46

Shonkoff, J. and Phillips, D. (2000) *From Neurons to Neighbourhoods: The Science of Early Childhood Development*, Washington, DC: National Academy Press

Showers, J. (2001) 'Preventing shaken baby syndrome', in Lazoritiz, S. and Palusci, V. (eds) (2001) *The Shaken Baby Syndrome – A Multidisciplinary Approach*, New York, NY: Haworth Maltreatment and Trauma Press

Sidebotham, P. and Fleming, P. (2007) *Unexpected Death in Childhood: A Handbook for Professionals*, Chichester, Sussex: Wiley

Sidebotham, P. and Golding, J. (2001) 'Child maltreatment in the "children of the nineties" – a longitudinal study of parental risk factors', *Child Abuse & Neglect*, Vol. 25, pp. 1177–200

Sidebotham, P. and Heron, J. (2006) 'Child maltreatment in the "children of the nineties": a longitudinal study of parental risk factors', *Child Abuse & Neglect*, Vol. 30, pp. 497–522

Smedslund, G., Dalsbø, T., Steiro, A., Winsvold, A. and Clench-Aas, J. (2011) 'Cognitive behavioural therapy for men who physically abuse their female partner', *Cochrane Database of Systematic Reviews*, Vol. 2

Smith, K. (2011) *Homicides, Firearms Offences and Intimate Violence r 2009/2010: Supplementary Volume 2 to Crime in England and Wales 2009/2010*, London: Home Office

Smith, M. (2004) 'Parental mental health: disruptions to parenting and outcomes for children', *Child and Family Social Work*, Vol. 9, pp. 3–11

Sousa, C., Herrenkohl, T. I., Moylan, C. A., Tajima, E. A., Klika, J. B., Herrenkohl, R. C. and Russo, M. J. (2011) 'Longitudinal study on the effects of child abuse and children's exposure to domestic violence, parent-child attachments, FHe and antisocial behaviour in adolescence', *Journal of Interpersonal Violence*, Vol. 26, pp. 111–36

Springer, K. W., Sheridan, J., Kuo, D. and Carnes, M. (2007) 'Long-term physical and mental health consequences of childhood physical abuse: results from a large population-based sample of men and women', *Child Abuse & Neglect*, Vol. 31, pp. 517–30

Stallard, P., Norman, P., Huline-Dickens, S., Salter, E. and Cribb, J. (2004) 'The effects of parental mental illness on children: a descriptive study of the views of parents and children', *Clinical Child Psychology and Psychiatry*, Vol. 9, pp. 39–52

Stanley, N., Ellis, J. and Bell, J. (2011a) 'Delivering preventative programmes in schools: identifying gender issues', in Barter, C. and Berridge, D. (eds) (2011) *Children Behaving Badly? Exploring Peer Violence Between Children and Young People*, London: Wiley

Stanley, N., Miller, P., Foster, H. R. and Thomson, G. (2011b) 'Children's experiences of domestic violence: developing an integrated response from police and child protection services', *Journal of Interpersonal Violence*, Vol. 20, pp. 1–20

Stanley, N., Penhal, E., Riordan, D., Barbour, R. S. and Holden, S. (2003) *Child Protection and Mental Health Services: Interprofessional Responses to the Needs of Mothers*, Bristol: Policy Press

Statham, J. (2004) 'Effective services to support children in special circumstances',

Child: Care, Health and Development, Vol. 30, pp. 589–98

Stein, A., Gath, D., Bucher J., Bond, A., Day, A. and Cooper. P, (1991) 'The relationship between postnatal depression and mother-child interaction', *British Journal of Psychiatry*, Vol. 158, pp. 46–52

Stewart, D. E. and Cecutti, A. (1993) 'Physical abuse in pregnancy', *Canadian Medical Association Journal*, Vol. 149, pp. 1257–63

Stith, S. M., Liu, T., Davies, L. C., Boykin, E. L., Alder, M. C., Harris, J. M., Som, A., McPherson, M. and Dees, J. (2009) 'Risk factors in child maltreatment: a meta-analytic review of the literature', *Aggression and Violent Behavior*, Vol. 14, pp. 13–29

Stokes, J. and Schmidt, G. (2012) Child protection decision-making: a factorial analysis using case vignettes', *Social Work*, Vol. 57, pp. 83–90

Straus, M. A., Gelles, R. J. and Smith, C. (1990) *Physical Violence in American Families: Risk Factors and Adaptations to Violence in 8,145 Families*, New Brunswick, NJ: Transaction Publishers

Straus, M. A., Hamby, S. L., Finkelhor, D., Moore, D. W. and Runyan, D. (1998) 'Identification of child maltreatment with the parent-child conflict tactics scales: development and psychometric data for a national sample of American parents', *Child Abuse & Neglect, Vol.* 22, pp. 249–70

Supkoff, L. M., Puig, J. and Sroufe, A. L. (2012) 'Situating resilience in developmental context', in Ungar, M. (ed.) (2012) *The Social Ecology of Resilience*, New York, NY: Springer, pp. 127–42

Sweet, M. A. and Appelbaum, M. I. (2004) 'Is home visiting an effective strategy? A metaanalytic review of home visiting programs for families with young children', *Child Development*, Vol. 75, pp. 1435–56

Taylor, J., Baldwin, N. and Spencer, N. (2008) 'Predicting child abuse and neglect: ethical, theoretical and methodological challenges', *Journal of Clinical Nursing*, Vol. 17, pp. 1193–200)

Taylor, J. and Redman, S. (2004) 'The smacking controversy: What advice should we be giving parents?', *Journal of Advanced Nursing*, Vol. 46, No. 3, pp. 311–18

Teicher, M. H. (2000) 'Wounds that time won't heal: the neurobiology of child abuse', *Cerebrum*, Vol. 2, pp. 50–67

Teicher, M. H., Dumont, N. L., Ito, Y., Vaituzis, C., Giedd, J. N. and Andersen, S. L. (2004) 'Childhood neglect is associated with reduced corpus callosum area', *Biological Psychiatry*, Vol. 56, pp. 80–5

Templeton, L., Zohhadi, S., Galvani, S. and Velleman, R. (2006) *'Looking Beyond Risk'. Parental Substance Misuse: Scoping Study*, Edinburgh: Scottish Executive. Available from URL: www.scotland.gov.uk/Publications/2006/07/05120121/0 (accessed 18 June 2014)

Thacker, S. B. and Stroup, D. F. (1998) 'Public health surveillance and health services research', in Armenian, H. K. and Shapiro, S. (eds) (1998) *Epidemiology and Health Services*, New York, NY: Oxford University Press, pp. 61–82

Thornberry, T. P., Knight, K. E. and Lovegrove, P. J. (2012) 'Does maltreatment beget maltreatment? A systematic review of the inter-generational literature', *Trauma, Violence, and Abuse*, Vol. 13, pp. 135–52

Thornberry, T. P., Knight, K. E. and Lovegrove, P. J. (2013) 'Adolescent risk factors for child maltreatment', *Child Abuse & Neglect, Vol. 38, No. 4, pp. 706–22*

Toth, S. L., Gravener-Davis, J. A., Guild, D. J. and Cicchetti, D. (2013) 'Relational interventions for child maltreatment: Past, present, and future perspectives', *Development and Psychopathology*, Vol. 4, No. 2, pp. 1601–17

Trevillion, K., Oram, S., Feder, G. and Howard, L. M. (2012) 'Experiences of domestic violence and mental disorders: a systematic review and meta-analysis', *PLOS ONE*, Vol. 7, e51740. doi:10.1371/journal.pone.0051740

Tunnard, J. (2004) *Parental Mental Health Problems: Key Messages from Research, Policy and Practice*, Dartington, Devon: Research in Practice

Turner, H. A., Finkelhor, D. and Ormrod, R. (2006) 'The effect of lifetime victimization on the mental health of children and adolescents', *Social Science and Medicine*, Vol. 62, pp. 13–27

Turner, H. A., Finkelhor, D. and Ormrod, R. (2010) 'Poly-victimization in a national sample of children and youth', *American Journal of Preventative Medicine*, Vol. 38, pp. 323–30

Twardosz, S. and Lutzker, J. R. (2010) 'Child maltreatment and the developing brain: a review of neuroscience perspectives', *Aggression and Violent Behavior*, Vol. 15, pp. 59–68

Ungar, M. (2008) 'Resilience across cultures", *British Journal of Social Work,* Vol. 38, pp. 218–35

Ungar, M. (2011) 'The social ecology of resilience. Addressing contextual and cultural ambiguity of a nascent construct', *American Journal of Orthopsychiatry*, Vol. 81, pp. 1–7

Ungar, M. (2012) *The Social Ecology of Resilience: A Handbook of Theory and Practice*, New York, NY: Springer

Ungar, M. (2013) 'Resilience after maltreatment: the importance of social services as facilitators of positive adaptation', *Child Abuse & Neglect, Vol 37*, pp. 110–15

UNICEF (2003) 'A league table of child maltreatment deaths in rich nations',(2003) *Innocenti Report Card 5*, Florence: UNICEF

Vary, J. (2000) *Young Parents in Gateshead … Life Now and Aspirations for 2000 and Beyond*, Gateshead: Gateshead Young Women's Outreach Project

Velleman, R. (1993) *Alcohol and the Family*, London: Institute of Alcohol Studies

Velleman, R. and Orford, J. (1999) *Risk and Resilience: Adults Who Were the Children of Problem Drinkers*, Amsterdam: Harwood Academic

Velleman, R., Templeton, L., Taylor, A. and Toner, P. (2003) *Evaluation of the Pilot Family Alcohol Service: Final Report*, Omaha, NE: Camelot Foundation

Vincent, S. (2010) 'Learning from child deaths and serious abuse', in Vincent, S. and Petch, A. (eds) (2010) *Audit and Analysis of Significant Case Reviews*, Edinburgh: Scottish Government

Vincent, S. and Petch, A. (2010) *Audit and Analysis of Significant Case Reviews*, Edinburgh: Scottish Government

Vinchon, M., Defoort-Dhellemmes, S., Desurmont, M. and Dhellemmes, P. (2005) 'Accidental and non-accidental head injuries in infants: A prospective study', *Journal of Neurosurgery*, Vol. 102, pp. 380–4

Walby, S. and Allen, J. (2004) *Domestic Violence, Sexual Assault and Stalking:*

Findings from the British Crime Survey, Home Office Research Study: 276, London: Home Office

Waldfogel, J. (2007) *Welfare Reforms and Child Well-Being in the US and UK,* London: CASE

Wallace, I. and Bunting, I. (2007) *An Examination of Local, National and International Arrangements for the Mandatory Reporting of Child Abuse,* Belfast: NSPCC

Walsh, C., MacMillan, H. and Jamieson, E. (2002) 'The relationship between parental psychiatric disorder and child physical and sexual abuse: findings from the Ontario Health Supplement', *Child Abuse & Neglect, Vol.* 26, pp. 11–22

Walsh, W. A., Dawson, J. and Mattingly, M. J. (2010) 'How are we measuring resilience following childhood maltreatment? Is the research adequate and consistent? What is the impact on research, practice, and policy?', *Trauma, Violence and Abuse,* Vol. 11, No. 1, pp. 27–41

Wassell, D. B. and Gilligan, R. (2010) *Child Development for Childcare and Protection Workers,* London: Jessica Kingsley

Webster-Stratton, C. (1990) 'Stress: a potential disruptor of parent perceptions and family interactions', *Journal of Clinical Child Psychology,* Vol. 19, pp. 302–12

Weniger, G., Lange, C., Sachsse, U. and Irle, E. (2008) 'Amygdala and hippocampal volumes and cognition in adult survivors of childhood abuse with dissociative disorders', *Acta Psychiatrica Scandinavia,* Vol. 118, pp. 281–90

West, S., Friedman, S. and Resnick, P. (2009) 'Fathers who kill their children; an analysis of the literature', *Journal of Forensic Science,* Vol. 54, pp. 463–8

Westmarland, N., Kelly, L. and Chalder-Mills, J. (2010) *Domestic Violence Perpetrator Programmes – What Counts as Success?,* London: Respect

Whittaker, A. and Elliott, L. (2010) 'Drug-using fathers', in Taylor, J. and Themessl-Huber, M. (eds) (2010) *Safeguarding Children in Primary Health Care,* London: Jessica Kingsley

Widom, C. S. (1989) 'Does violence beget violence? A critical examination of the literature', *Psychological Bulletin,* Vol. 106, pp. 3–28

Widom, C. S. (1999) 'Post-traumatic stress disorder in abused and neglected children grown up', *American Journal of Psychiatry,* Vol. 156, pp. 1223–9

Widom, C. S. and Maxfield, M. G. (2001) *An Update on the 'Cycle of Violence',* Washington, DC: National Institute of Justice

Williams, Z. (2014) 'Is misused neuroscience defining early years and child protection policy?', *The Guardian.* Available from URL: www.theguardian.com/ education/2014/apr/26/misused-neuroscience-defining-child-protection- policy (accessed 18 June 2014)

Wolfe, D. A., Crooks, C. V., Lee, V., MacIntyre-Smith, A. and Jaffe, P. G. (2003) 'The effects of children's exposure to domestic violence: a meta-analysis and critique', *Clinical Child and Family Psychology Review,* Vol. 6, pp. 171–87

Women and Equality Unit. (2003) *Increasing Safe Accommodation Choices,* London: The Stationery Office.

Woodman, J., Brandon, M., Bailey, S., Belderson, P., Sidebotham, P. and Gilbert, R. (2011) 'Healthcare use by children fatally or seriously harmed by child maltreatment: analysis of a national case series 2005–2007', *Archives of Disease in Childhood*, Vol. 96, pp. 270–5

Woolfall, K., Sumnall, H. and McVeigh, J. (2008) *Addressing the Needs of Children of Substance Using Parents: An Evaluation of Families First's Intensive Intervention: Final Report.* Liverpool: Liverpool John Moores University

World Health Organization (2008) *Eliminating Female Genital Mutilation: An Interagency Statement*, Geneva: World Health Organization

World Health Organization/London School of Hygiene and Tropical Medicine (2010) *Preventing Intimate Partner Violence and Sexual Violence Against Women: Taking Action and Generating Evidence*, Geneva: World Health Organization/London School of Hygiene and Tropical Medicine

Wright, M. O. and Masten, A. S. (2005) 'Resilience processes in development: Fostering positive adaptation in the context of adversity', in Goldstein, S. and Brooks, R. B. (eds) (2005) *Handbook of Resilience in Children*, New York, NY: Springer, pp. 17–37

Wu, G., Feder, A., Cohen, H., Kim, J. J., Calderon, S., Charney, D. S. and Mathe, A. A. (2013) 'Understanding resilience', *Front Behavioural Science*, Vol. 7, pp. 1–15

Wyszynski, M. (1999) 'Shaken baby syndrome: Identification, intervention, and prevention', *Clinical Excellence in Nursing Practice*, Vol. 3, No. 5, pp. 262–7

Zohhadi, Sarah, Templeton, Lorna and Velleman, Richard (2006) *Clouds Families Plus: An Evaluation Report*, Bath: University of Bath, Mental Health Research and Development Unit

INDEX

Note: page numbers in *italics* denote figures